ENGLISH FOLK-HEROES

"Communicable Relics"

ENGLISH FOLK-HEROES

By
CHRISTINA HOLE

Illustrated from Original Woodcuts
By ERIC KING

DORSET PRESS
NEW YORK

This edition published by Dorset Press,
a division of Marboro Books Corp.

1992 Dorset Press

ISBN 0-88029-721-2

Printed and bound in the United States of America

M 9 8 7 6 5 4 3 2 1

CONTENTS

FOREWORD

IN this book a brief attempt has been made to record the principal legends of some of our national folk-heroes, and to relate these legends to the true facts of their lives, as far as they are known. Of the many folk-heroes of English tradition, only a few are mentioned here, since in so short a book it would obviously have been impossible to do justice to them all. Those who are included have been chosen for two reasons. All are true folk-heroes inasmuch as they live in folklore as well as in history, and are the subjects of numerous legends, ballads and stories handed down from generation to generation. And all are either known to be authentic historical characters, or are people who may reasonably be supposed to have existed, in spite of the dense fog of magic or of miracle which has gathered round them in the course of centuries.

The most doubtful from an historical point of view are, of course, Arthur and Robin Hood. The existence of both has been questioned by many writers, though most modern historians now incline to the view that Arthur, or someone like him, led the British resistance in the fifth century, and not a few are willing to concede the possibility of a genuine Robin Hood. They are both included here, not only because they are amongst the greatest of our national heroes, but also because I believe that when due allowance has been made for the scarcity of reliable evidence and the distorting effect of folk-legend and poetical romance, there is a strong probability that their traditions sprang in the first instance from memories of real men whose life-stories, however heavily embroidered later, bore some resemblance in the main to the legends afterwards handed down from father to son.

The men and women in this book were all widely known in their own day and continued to exercise great influence after their deaths. I have not been able to record the lives of purely local heroes, nor have I been able, for reasons of space, to include many who were born at a comparatively late date in our history.

FOREWORD

Such men as Nelson, Prince Rupert, Cromwell or Lord Derwent-water do not appear here, though all were folk-heroes in the true sense inasmuch as they were passionately admired leaders in their own and later times, and have each become the subject of many folk-legends. Again, many noble names are necessarily missing because their owners, though undoubtedly great, apparently did not possess that elusive and indefinable quality which fires the imagination of ordinary people, and without which no man can hope to become a hero of the folk. That quality, like genius, appears in unexpected quarters, and is often absent where it might be most confidently expected. If one may judge by their several places in folk-tradition, many brave and gallant men did not possess it, and several scoundrels seem to have had it; the roll of folk-heroes contains some very odd names, and the omissions from it are as curious as the inclusions.

I am indebted for much kindness to many librarians, clergymen and others who have allowed me to see scarce books, or have told me of heroic traditions current in their own localities. To these, and particularly to my friend, Miss J. M. Eltenton, who read each chapter as it was written, made many excellent suggestions and criticisms, and also corrected the proofs, I offer my sincere and genuine thanks for their ungrudging and very valuable help.

Oxford   CHRISTINA HOLE

CHAPTER I

THE HERO LEGEND

EVERY nation has its real or mythical heroes, whose deeds are chronicled in song, ballad and story and whose legends form part of the national heritage of history and folk-lore. Such legends are at once the most popular and the most persistent of all folk-tales. They are frequently founded, at least in part, upon fact; they are full of stirring incidents and are nearly always interesting. They are connected with places well known to their hearers and with people whose names have long been household words. They enshrine the most cherished traditions of the race to which they belong, and are handed down from generation to generation as a proof of what that race could once do and may in the future do again. Among primitive peoples they often concern the gods who walked among men in the beginning of time, and thus have a religious sanction; in later stages of civilization they chronicle the deeds of real men and women, or of those eponymous, and usually fictitious, individuals who gave their names to tribes or places, as the Trojan Brutus did to Britain, or King Lud to London.

Stories of human heroes naturally have the strongest hold upon the minds of their hearers. The Culture Gods who descend from Heaven to teach their people the arts of life are remembered for so long as their cult persists. But at the best they are remote beings from another world, and with the changing of faiths they fade from memory, and their story becomes a mere nursery-tale whose real meaning is forgotten or only half understood. The human hero, on the other hand, strikes a perennial chord in every man's heart. He represents in himself all those self-conscious aspirations which even the dullest sometimes feel, and is what each one of us secretly hopes he might be, should the occasion ever arise. An advanced and cultivated people which has long since relegated its *Marchen* to the nursery will still listen appreciatively to its sagas of great men, even though it rejects their marvellous details, and sometimes the very foundations of the tales, as fabulous. So in England the names of Arthur and St. George, Hereward the Wake and Lady Godiva still have power to stir our imagination, though some of the stories concerning them are quite incredible and are borrowed directly from pagan or fairy mythology. Their virtues survive to this day as a moral force, and their legends, even while we question them in detail or in essence, are as carefully handed on from parent to child as ever they were in less critical ages.

Story-telling is a universal instinct. Children demand stories at an early age, and the young child, like his primitive adult ancestor, usually insists that the same tale shall be repeated without alterations and as nearly as possible in the same words every time. The professional story-teller never lacked an audience, whether his tales were recounted for pure amusement, or in an attempt to explain the phenomena of nature or the facts of history. By stories primitive man sought to account for his own existence and that of the world around him; in tales and ballads his descendants preserved the records of their race and the glorious or doleful traditions of their past. When reading was the privilege of the few and entertainment was comparatively rare, listening to old and well-tried tales was the principal pleasure of long winter evenings, as it still is in remote regions to-day. And of all the stories that were told at such gatherings of listeners, those which could be believed and which fired the mind to admiration, pity, or vicarious pride were always the most popular and most constantly demanded. Into this class came the hero-legends. They are probably much older than the purely imaginative tale, for just as young children like to think a story is true, however marvellous its details, so did our early ancestors. The sagas had the great merit of being concerned in most cases with real people and places, though they were usually enriched by gems of the story-teller's fancy and the incorporation of incidents already well known and recounted many times before of other men or gods who lived and fought farther back in time.

For us the principal interest of these legends lies in the historical facts they often contain, and the mirror they hold up to the ideas and beliefs current at the time when the tales were first told. Ancient beliefs everywhere colour the simple records with wonder and marvels, and in many cases so obscure the true facts as to render doubtful not only the actions but, as in the case of Arthur, the very existence of the man about whom they centre. The hero may have been, and frequently was, a genuine historical personage whose exploits were sufficiently remarkable to ensure remembrance without extraneous additions. High courage, steadfastness, force of will and simple good luck may afford all the explanation needed to account for his success or the grandeur of his failure, for these qualities belong to all ages and are fortunately less rare than is sometimes supposed. But to the people of his day, and more particularly to their successors who knew the hero only when the glamour of the past already lay over him, he often seemed something more than a man. His prowess could be explained for them only by the intervention of fairies and spirits, or by fairy or divine descent. Magicians aided him in his difficulties; fairies presided at his birth, or a fairy wife instructed him in the arts of war and leadership, and so raised him above the general level of mankind. Or the high gods were listed among his ancestors, remote or immediate, and this divine kinship endowed him with superhuman courage, and enabled him to perform more splendid deeds than ordinary mortals could achieve.

In pagan religious thought the boundaries between Heaven and Earth were less rigid than they subsequently became under Christianity, and even in comparatively advanced civilizations the

3

idea of divine descent presented no particular difficulties. There was nothing inherently impossible in a union between gods and mortals, and the descendants of such marriages, though human, were usually something more than ordinary. The kingship everywhere was closely associated with divinity. The primitive priest-kings were incarnations of the gods; the later kings of heathendom were descended from them. The Irish kings sprang from the Tuatha de Danann, who were gods before they became the fairies of Ireland; in Wales the blood of the Children of Don ran in the veins of the early princes. The pagan rulers of Scandinavia, Germany and England were all of divine lineage, and even the Christian Alfred was not ashamed to trace his ancestry back to the high gods of northern Europe and claim direct descent from Woden, Sceaf and Geat.

After the coming of Christianity, this heavenly kinship was often disguised by traditions of fairy birth, or descent from some legendary hero who had once been worshipped as a god. The ancient divinities were dethroned when the nations were converted, but they did not die. They survived as demons or as fairies, and sometimes as far-off kings who were possessed of magical powers. Bran the Blessed was once a Celtic god, but he reappears in the Welsh Triads as a virtuous king who brought Christianity to his kingdom, and was one of "the three blissful Rulers of the Island of Britain." When he was about to die of a poisoned wound, he commanded his followers to cut off his head and bury it in the White Tower of London, with the face towards France. For so long as it remained there, Britain would be safe from invasion from Europe. His friends carried the severed head about with them for eighty years, during which the birds of Rhiannon sang to them, and they were unconscious of the passage of time. Eventually the head was brought to London and buried as the hero desired, and there it remained until Arthur removed it, wishing to hold his kingdom by his own strength alone.

What is more to our purpose in his legend is that the Triads call him the father of Caradoc, or Caratacus, who led the Britons against the armies of Ostorius. We know from Dio Cassius that Caradoc was, in fact, the son of Cunobelinus, the ruler of south-eastern Britain, whose capital was at Colchester. His heroic

Caractacus: Hero in Defeat

5

struggle against heavy odds impressed the Romans who defeated him almost as much as it did the Britons. Tacitus tells us that "his fame had travelled far beyond those islands; it had reached the adjoining provinces and even spread through Italy. People longed to see what man it was that for so many years had defied the power of Rome. His name was great in Rome itself; and Caesar, in exalting his own glory, enhanced that of his fallen foe." And he adds that when the British leaders were led in triumph through Rome, "the others dishonoured themselves by craven supplications, but not so Caratacus, who abated nothing of his high looks, and made no appeal for mercy."[1]

In the Welsh legend this historical leader has become confused with the mythological Caradoc, whose father was Bran the god. But Bran himself had suffered a change in the course of years, and from a war-god had become a noble king who shared his heroic son's captivity and afterwards converted his people to Christianity. There is no evidence that this change preserves the memory of any real King Bran, and even if such a man existed in the time of Ostorius, we know that he was not Caradoc's father, nor was he in Rome with him. Tacitus says that Caradoc's wife, daughter and brothers were his fellow-captives, but he does not mention his father. Cunobelinus certainly could not have been there, for he was already dead. It seems clear that the saintly king of the Triads is simply the old god in a new form; a confusion of names has made the historical Caradoc his son, and by thus endowing the hero with a once-divine father the chroniclers have provided an easy and, to them, natural explanation of his great courage and integrity.

Aine, the mother of Earl Gerald, the Irish hero, is said to have been a fairy, but it is probable that she was originally the mother-goddess, Anu, whose name is perpetuated in the two Kerry mountains called the Paps of Anu. Unlike many Irish fairies, she was kind-hearted and friendly to mankind. She protected cattle and crops, and drove away the demons who brought disease to men and animals. She was also associated with fire-worship, and on St. John's Eve the people of Knockainy used, until recently, to go in procession round the fairy hill in which she lived, carrying

[1] Tacitus, *Annals*, Bk. XII.

flaming torches and burning wisps of straw which were afterwards taken through the fields and byres to bring fertility to the farms. Tradition says that once when they neglected this ceremony the hill burst into flame of itself.

From this divine or fairy mother the Earl learnt those arts of sorcery by which he won his victories and which, according to one story, betrayed him in the end and were the cause of his long enchantment. He had the power of turning himself into birds or animals at will. His wife greatly desired to see this change, and he agreed to show her, on condition that she made no sound or sign of alarm throughout the proceedings. He warned her that if she did so, he would never regain his human shape until generations of men were under the soil. He then changed himself into a goldfinch. A hawk pursued him, and his wife could not refrain from crying out in terror. The goldfinch flew away, and since that time the Earl has not been seen in this world. But, as we shall see, another story makes him one of the sleeping heroes of Ireland, who rides out once in seven years and will reappear at the appointed time to deliver the country from her enemies for ever.

The famous physicians of Myddrai were descended from the Lady of Llyn y Van Vach, who is called a fairy in Welsh folktales, but seems rather to have been a local water-goddess or spirit. She rose from the lake to marry the farmer of Esgair Llaethoy, and thither she returned with all her flocks and herds when her husband had broken the tabu imposed upon him at the time of his wedding. To her eldest son, Rhiwallon, she imparted the secrets of medical lore, and from him sprang a long line of healers and herbalists, whose curious skill was transmitted from generation to generation until the beginning of the nineteenth century. A book of their recipes is still in existence. It was compiled in the thirteenth century, and contains some prescriptions which certainly date back to the time of Howel the Good, as well as others which are believed to be of sixth-century origin.

The fairy wife or mistress occurs in many hero-tales. Charles the Great, who had a fairy ancestress named Berhta, loved a strange woman at Aix who lived only when he was with her and died when he departed. One day he saw the sunlight glinting on a grain of gold on her tongue. He took it from her, and she fell dead at his feet, never to be revived again. Wild Edric had a fairy wife who left him when he reminded her of her alien kin. Thomas the Rhymer lived in Fairyland for three years, and from its Queen received his powers of prophecy and the perhaps more doubtful gift of being unable to tell a lie. On the last day of his earthly life he was feasting at Earlston when a message reached him that a hart and a hind were walking down the village street. He arose at once and followed them, and was never seen again, except by the few who claimed to have seen him resting, like Arthur, in an enchanted sleep under the Eildon Hills.

Sometimes the hero's achievements were ascribed simply to his own knowledge of witchcraft. Owen Glendower was regarded as a powerful sorcerer both by his followers and by his enemies. He possessed a magic stone which fell from the body of a raven owned by the Earl of Arundel, and which had the power of making its owner invisible. He was able to raise storms and winds at will, and three times hampered and defeated the English forces by this means. In 1402 Henry IV's army was almost destroyed by violent tempests which swept over Wales throughout August and September. On September 8th the King's own tent was blown down and his lance hurled through the air on to his body; had he not been sleeping in his armour he must inevitably have been killed.

Jack Cade in 1450 was accused of using books of magic to secure the success of his rebellion and of raising the Devil in the form of a black dog at his lodgings in Dartford. Though this accusation was brought by his enemies, it is quite possible that his followers also credited him with magical powers, though, viewed from their angle, these would, of course, be concerned with white magic alone. Oliver Cromwell was supposed by Royalists to have made a compact with the Devil for a term of years and to have been carried away by the fiend on the night of his death, 3 September 1658. The fierce storm which then raged was believed to be of the Devil's raising. The Roundheads, for their part, whilst attributing their leader's success to God's will and his own merits, asserted that Prince Rupert's great military skill was due to witchcraft. It was generally believed by those on the Puritan side that his favourite dog, Boy, who went everywhere with him and was killed at

Marston Moor, was his familiar spirit and spied for him upon the opposing armies.

Heroes often became the heirs of gods, fairies and giants in other ways than by simple descent. As ancient cults were abandoned and gradually forgotten, their surviving beliefs and legends were frequently attached to famous men, into whose story were woven incidents to account for age-old superstitions or still-continued customs whose original religious meaning had been forgotten. Undying heroes slept in the former homes of gods and fairies and sometimes assumed their functions. The rocky Beds, Cups and Drinking Troughs that once belonged to the giants of antiquity were inherited by later heroes, some of whom, like Robin Hood, also acquired their power of hurling enormous boulders over great distances and leaving the marks of their fingers upon solid rocks. Ancient water-spirits who lurked in dangerous pools and rivers occasionally reappeared as ghosts of once-living men, like the nixie who must formerly have lived in the pool on the Swale now known as Hoggett's Hole. There Thomas Hoggett, a highwayman, was drowned in the eighteenth century whilst escaping from the watch. His ghost haunted the pool and has since drowned many; local tradition says that no one who falls into this dangerous water ever escapes, no matter how strong a swimmer he may be. There can be little doubt that Hoggett's ghost is but a later form of the pool's indwelling spirit, one of the great company of such spirits whom our forefathers saw in every lake and river and who, like Jenny Greenteeth in Lancashire and Peg Powler in the Tees, was frequently inimical to mankind.

One of the most persistent pagan superstitions was the tradition of the Wild Hunt, that terrible band of hounds and men which rode through the night and brought death or misfortune to all who beheld it. In northern Europe Woden was its original leader, but long after his name had ceased to awe men's minds the Hunt he led continued to pass through the darkness and to leave its trail of fear. His place was taken by a diversity of famous men, by Arthur, King Herla and Wild Edric in England, by Earl Gerald in Ireland, by Hugh Capet or Herod in France. Sometimes indeed the old god still rode out thinly disguised as the Devil in pursuit of human souls, or harrying the ghosts of the sinful dead. In

Cornwall the unjust magistrate, Tregeagle, fled over the moors before the Devil's hounds; in Norfolk Sir Thomas Boleyn drove every year in a spectral coach over forty county bridges, pursued by a pack of demon dogs. But usually the leader was some once-renowned hero, or even a local celebrity unknown beyond the boundaries of his own district.

Men of violent character, and those who came to a sudden end, were often associated with the Wild Hunt. In 1604 Sir Walter Calverley killed two of his children and attempted to kill his wife in a fit of mania. Harassed by debt, unfounded jealousy, and the consequences of a wild life, his mind suddenly gave way, but his insanity was only temporary. When he recovered, he refused to plead at his trial, in order to save his estates for the remaining child. The consequence of such a refusal was death by pressing, and this horrible fate he resolutely suffered. His ghost haunted his house in the usual manner, but it also raged through the countryside at the head of a band of spectres, and mercilessly rode down all who crossed his path. Here once again, in this remote Yorkshire district, more than a thousand years after the intro-duction of Christianity, is the ancient pagan Hunt in all its savagery. The god's place has been taken by an unhappy ghost associated in local memory with bloodshed and violence, as in other parts of England it was taken by other notable men or even, in some cases, by a vague tradition of an unknown M.F.H. who hunted on Sunday, or was destroyed by his own hounds.

Sir Francis Drake used to be seen riding over Dartmoor in a black coach, followed by a pack of hounds whose cry instantly killed every dog that heard it. The spectral coach was the direct descendant of the Wild Hunt, and in the transitional stage of the superstition its ghostly occupant was often accompanied or pursued by demon dogs. Sir Francis was a man universally admired and loved, the champion of his country and a benefactor to his native town and county, yet the Devonians saw nothing inappropriate in his journeyings in so ominous a vehicle. Round this comparatively modern admiral gathered a host of stories as marvellous as any that had been told of the legendary heroes of the past. He could see things happening thousands of miles away; he could hurl heavy objects over distances never attempted by the ancient giants.

During one of his long absences from England his wife, supposing herself a widow, planned to marry again. From the other side of the world Drake saw her standing with his rival before the altar and seizing a cannon-ball he threw it with such unerring aim that it fell between the couple without harming either. Death itself was not sufficient to extinguish so bright a spirit, and he became an undying hero, ready to return to England's aid if his drum at Buckland Abbey was sounded. One curious tradition links him directly with the old Celtic god, Manannan, son of Ler. This god by magic could make chips of wood thrown into the sea appear like ships of war. Legend says that Drake was once sitting on the Devil's Point at Plymouth whittling a stick. As the shavings fell into the water below him, they turned into full-sized ships, not mere glamorous appearances like those of Manannan, but real vessels, fully rigged and ready for action whenever their creator and master should require them.

Lady Godiva is principally remembered for her famous ride through Coventry, which was annually commemorated in that city by a procession during the Great Fair in Trinity Week, in which the Mayor, Aldermen and City Guilds took part. She was the wife of Earl Leofric of Mercia, grandmother of the famous earls, Edwin and Morcar, and co-foundress with her husband of the Benedictine monastery in Coventry in which both were afterwards buried. Tradition says she was both beautiful and pious, renowned for her charity and beloved of all the people of Leofric's wide territories. The well-known legend concerning her states that in her time Coventry was oppressed by heavy tolls and other exactions imposed by her husband and that, in order to free the town from these burdens, she consented to ride naked through the streets in daylight. As a reward for this act of singular devotion the Earl remitted the tolls and granted a charter of exemption to the people for ever.

This curious story seems to have no foundation whatever in historical fact, but to have sprung from some dimly remembered fertility rite once celebrated in that district and later associated with a real woman already beloved for her charity and benevolence. It is not recorded by the early chroniclers who mention Godiva or Leofric. It is first told by Roger of Wendover who wrote in the thirteenth century, about a hundred and fifty years after her death. He tells us that "The countess Godiva, who was a great lover of God's mother, longing to free the town of Coventry from the oppression of a heavy toll, often with urgent prayers besought her husband that from regard to Jesus Christ and His mother, he would free the town from that service and from all other heavy burdens." The Earl refused and forbade her to mention the matter again, but she continued to make her request until, in perhaps pardonable exasperation, he promised to grant her wish if she would ride naked "before all the people, through the market of the town, from one end to the other." To this extraordinary suggestion, so alien both to Leofric's known character and the customs of the time, she agreed. "Whereupon," says Roger, "the countess, beloved of God, loosed her hair and let down her tresses which covered the whole of her body like a veil, and then mounting her horses and attended by two knights, she rode through the market place without being seen, except for her fair legs; and having completed the journey, she returned with gladness to her astonished husband and obtained of him what she had asked, for Earl Leofric freed the town of Coventry and its inhabitants from the aforesaid service, and confirmed what he had done by a charter."[1]

In this early version of the legend there is no mention of any command laid upon the people to remain indoors, or of Peeping Tom who afterwards became an important part of the story. Such a command, in fact, would scarcely agree with the Earl's barbarous condition, which was that she should ride naked "before all the people". Later tradition says, however, that when he realized his wife was serious in her intention, Leofric ordered the inhabitants of the town to close their windows and doors and to refrain from looking outside during the Countess's ride upon pain of death. All obeyed except one man, a tailor, who peeped from an upper window as she passed his house, and was immediately struck blind by the wrath of Heaven.

In this supernatural punishment we have, perhaps, an indication of the religious origin of the story. We are reminded at once of those strange ceremonies of heathendom in which only women

[1] Roger of Wendover, *Flores Historiarum.*

13

took part and from which men were rigorously excluded. Nothing in the history of Coventry suggests that the legend preserves the memory of any real event. In Godiva's time the town was little more than a village, containing some 350 inhabitants, few of whom were above the rank of serfs, and lacking any market of a size sufficient to make the tolls of importance to its overlord. Moreover, it is not the only legend of its kind in England. At St. Briavels in Gloucestershire bread and cheese are annually distributed on Whit-Sunday after the evening service, in commemoration of certain rights variously said to have been granted by King John or by an unspecified Earl of Herefordshire. These rights included the gathering of wood in Hudnolls, and Samuel Rudder tells us in his *History of Gloucestershire* that the Earl's wife obtained this privilege for the people by a ride similar to that of Lady Godiva. It will be noticed that in both cases an important benefit for the people in general was gained through the lady's unusual action, and its commemoration takes the form of a communal ceremony—a municipal parade in the city, a shared feast in the village.

At Southam, formerly a procession was held in which two figures were carried, both representing Lady Godiva. One of these was black. The custom has now lapsed completely, and no one knows for certain what meaning was attached to this black figure by those who carried her. The inhabitants of Southam, though they lived in Leofric's territory, could not have shared in any privileges gained by Coventry, and there is no reason to suppose that the procession commemorated any event in the history of the village. Probably the black figure was much older than its companion. It may have represented some archaic goddess of fertility to whom Lady Godiva's name was only later attached. Or it may have had some connexion with those rites, which Pliny mentions but does not describe, in which British women and girls took part with their unclothed bodies stained almost to blackness by woad.

In early thought nakedness had great power in itself, and was used in the ceremonies of many religions and in magic. Women could avert storms by exposing themselves, or ensure plentiful crops by harnessing themselves naked to the plough and drawing it over the fields. Fertility could be promoted by rites in which the participants went unclothed, and mediaeval witches, who could both blast and foster it, were popularly supposed to uncover themselves during parts of the Sabbat. Rogers in his *Social Life of Scotland* mentions a custom in which boys, who seem here to have taken the place of priests or women, ran naked round a mound known as the King's Knot, in Stirling, at the beginning of May, and sometimes at midsummer and Lammas as well. It seems clear that, since the rides of Lady Godiva and the Countess of Hereford have no certain historical foundation, their legends must have arisen from some ancient custom which survived in Warwickshire and Gloucestershire long after the fertility cult from which it sprang was dead. When all that remained in human memory of its meaning was a vague tradition of communal good proceeding from the nakedness of women, explanatory legends arose which, in Coventry and Southam, centred round the revered name of Lady Godiva, and at St. Briavels round that of a less clearly remembered Countess of Hereford, who may once have been the benefactress of her people in some more usual manner.

Hero-legends are not, as a rule, democratic in outlook. Unlike nursery tales, they are not usually concerned with poor men who rose to eminence, but with men of noble and, as we have seen, sometimes divine lineage, who were leaders by right of birth as well as by right of merit. Many historical heroes were, in fact, men of high position, and those who were not have often had rank and fortune ascribed to them by chroniclers in later times. Arthur has become a king in tradition, though there is little or no reason for supposing that he was one in fact. Robin Hood, whose ancestry is extremely uncertain, is usually said to have been the Earl of Huntingdon, or at least to have had legitimate claims to that title. The few heroes of lowly birth who appear as they really were in legends seem to be an exception to the general rule. For the most part, the passionate admiration of their followers, coupled with the romantic fancies of chroniclers, demands that the great man should be great in every way, and that to his admitted virtues should be added ancient blood and an hereditary right to the loyalty of those he leads.

One of the few instances of the opposite tendency in English hero-tales occurs in the story of Dick Whittington. In the famous legend he appears as a poor boy who was driven by the extreme poverty of his parents to seek employment in London. There he took a menial post in Alderman Fitzwarren's house, and was so cruelly treated by the cook that he ran away and only returned when he heard Bow Bells ringing out their prophecy of his prosperous future. The Alderman allowed all his servants to venture their property in his trading ships, and Dick entrusted him with his only possession, a cat. Through this excellent mouser he made a fortune which enabled him to marry his employer's daughter, and eventually to become three times Mayor of London, as well as Member of Parliament for the city.

The latter part of this romantic story is true, for he did marry Alice Fitzwarren, and he was Mayor in 1397, 1406 and 1419. Much argument has centred round the incident of the cat, some writers considering it to be based at least partially upon fact, and others asserting that it arose from a corruption of the French word *achat*, a purchase, or from the name "cat", then applied to coal-ships. Neither of these explanations is very convincing; the second is particularly weak, for coal-ships at that period were called hoys, and as Whittington was a silk merchant in later life, it is unlikely that his fortune was founded upon coal. The story itself is told of other men and is a widespread folk-tale found in many countries. Nevertheless, it is possible that Whittington may have had some connexion with cats, if only that of a marked affection for these intelligent and delightful creatures. In the foundations of a fifteenth-century house built by one of his relatives a sculptured stone was discovered which showed him with a cat in his arms, and this may commemorate either one of his personal characteristics or some tradition of his family. Such a connexion, if known, would afford ample scope for embroideries, and would probably be sufficient to account for the inclusion of an already well-known story concerning cats among the many tales told about the popular merchant.

But whatever the true solution of the cat mystery may be, there is no doubt that the legend of Whittington's lowly origin is false. He was the son of Sir William Whittington and was born at Pauntley, where his arms and those of Alice Fitzwarren are in the

west window of the church. In 1371 or 1373 he was apprenticed
to Sir John Fitzwarren, according to the custom of the time. No
doubt he endured some hardships during his seven years' appren-
ticeship, for it was a rough age in which the happiness of children
was little considered, but his was not a menial position, and it is
unlikely that he was seriously ill-treated in the mercer's house. In
due course he became a member of the Mercers' Company and a
very wealthy man, highly respected for his integrity and his
benevolence.

Merchants are not usually romantic figures, and few have received
the honour of being ranked with folk-heroes in the popular mind.
But Whittington seems to have been something more than an
ordinary trader and to have deserved more than most the title of
merchant prince. His charity was boundless. He built libraries
and almshouses, restored St. Bartholomew's Hospital, endowed a
college, provided a water-tap for thirsty wayfarers in Cripplegate.
He put down abuses among the City Companies and boldly
attacked the powerful Brewers' Company for selling dear ale;
during one of his mayoralties he summarily forbade the practice of
sending fur-cap makers' apprentices to scour caps in the Thames
during bitterly cold or stormy weather. He subscribed large sums
to equip troops for the war in Scotland and, on one occasion,
showed himself capable of those grand gestures which fire the public
imagination in all ages. When Henry V borrowed £60,000 from
the City Companies to finance the French war, Whittington bought
up the bonds and, whilst entertaining the King at a banquet,
threw them into the fire, thus releasing the King from a heavy debt.

Nor were all his benefactions of this public character. Once,
when he was Sheriff in 1394, a young man just out of his appren-
ticeship was sued by his former master for an error of judgment
which had involved his employer in loss. Being unable to pay
either the original debt or the damages, he was thrown into prison.
For his safe custody Whittington, as Sheriff, was responsible, and
when, five months later, it was found that the lad was no longer
in prison the master claimed debt and damages from Whittington.
The latter did not contest the action but paid the large sum
involved without protest. Later it was learnt that, being convinced
the prisoner had committed no moral wrong and was the victim

of misfortune only, he had deliberately allowed him to go free and make a fresh start, though he was well aware what the consequences of his action would be. Such stories naturally endeared him to the people of London, and they rewarded him unconsciously by raising him to the rank of a folk-hero and embroidering his life-history with ancient tales, thus conferring on him an honour more enduring than any of the kings of his time could give.

CHAPTER II

THE UNDYING HERO

THE most persistent and widely distributed of all the marvellous tales that gather round the memory of great men is that of the undying hero, the man whom death has not defeated and who is separated from his people only by a temporary enchantment. It is found in all countries and in all ages, wherever men have placed great faith and trust in a particular leader and have looked confidently to him for protection and guidance. The folk-lore of innumerable nations, including our own, is starred with the names of men who once led their people to victory and whose deaths were followed by a widespread belief that they were not really dead, but sleeping in some spiritual or earthly resting-place whence they would return after the lapse of a certain period. Such men were the dreamt-of deliverers who, at their second coming, would finally defeat the enemies of their country and inaugurate a long period of peace and prosperity. Occasionally it was the incarnate god of the tribe who was thus expected, but more usually it was some historical or semi-historical character whose exploits had made a deep impression upon his contemporaries, and whose death represented an irreparable loss to the cause for which he fought. It is precisely this death which the legends everywhere deny; the hero has left his people for a time, but he is still living and he will come again in the day of their gravest peril. The nature of his temporary dwelling varies with the age of the legend, but in every case the central point of the tale is the denial of final extinction and the firm belief that the link between the leader and the led has not been severed for ever, even though it may in some mysterious way have been interrupted for a time.

That such a belief should be so widespread and so persistent is not entirely surprising, for it had its roots in man's eternal resistance to disaster, and his instinctive faith that goodness and strength cannot finally be overcome by evil. It was fed continually by that protective mechanism of the mind which refuses to credit unhappy tidings or admit defeat, and by the love of the marvellous which has existed in all ages. It was nourished by oppression and strengthened by a confused feeling that one who had proved stronger than his enemies in life might also be strong enough to defeat even death itself and somehow escape the common doom of man. Amongst oppressed and struggling peoples it was a firm support in present trouble and an incentive to further resistance to tyranny. In the darkest periods of their history it was often their main bulwark against despair and served to keep alight the fire of courage in hearts which had no other source of hope.

In its simplest form the legend describes the hero as sleeping in a cave or mountain in his own country, or in some locality with which he was connected in life. Thus he is still in this world and can even be seen upon occasion by those bold enough to penetrate to his secret fastness. His horses are watered in local streams and exercised in local by-ways; if one dies or is lost, it is sometimes replaced by a living horse acquired by purchase or other means from a nearby farmer. Food is served at his table, and in some stories a housekeeper or steward buys wheaten bread daily over a long period of time from a baker of the district. The hero's sleep is not perpetual or uninterrupted. He may stir at seven-year intervals, or be roused by the sound of music or the voice of an intruder. Sometimes he rides out with his followers and is seen

The Hero in the Mountains

21

by benighted wayfarers, and he or his steward frequently talk with ordinary human beings and reward visitors with material gifts.

But in spite of these evidences of his humanity he is easily confused with the gods and fairies associated with his mountain dwelling, and in the course of time he often acquires some of their more marvellous attributes. His beard grows easily through a stone table; his strength is far beyond that of other men. His cavern is brilliantly lit, though it is far below the earth's surface and there are no visible torches to light it. He is often the guardian of vast treasures which lie in gleaming heaps before him and from which visitors to his dwelling are allowed to help themselves. Or apparently valueless gifts received at his hands turn into gold before the recipients reach their homes. Occasionally those who visit him find that years have passed in the course of what they thought was but a short stay, or that some minor disobedience to his command is followed by disproportionate punishment. In some cases his dwelling is clearly connected with the land of the dead, and those who enter it are never seen again in this world. Usually, however, the sleeping hero is less terrifying than the spirits he resembles, and to see him brings no immediate evil to the beholder, as does the sight of the high gods. His enchantment can sometimes be broken by blowing a bugle or drawing a sword found in the cavern. Many folk-tales recount the experiences of those who tried to waken him thus and failed at the last moment through lack of courage. But his final return is not dependent upon any human action, for it is ordained that he will come again at the appointed time and deliver his people for good and all from the power of their enemies.

This is the oldest and most general form of this ancient belief, with all its clearly marked traces of paganism and primitive thought. In more advanced stages of civilization the details are less materialistic, though the underlying idea is the same. The hero no longer sleeps on earth or holds converse with those still living in this world. He is in Paradise, or in some far country where no man can follow him. But he still watches over his own land and will return when he is most needed. The stories of Arthur and Ogier the Dane mark a transitional stage between the older and newer versions of the legend, for both these heroes were variously said to live in Avalon and in earthly caverns. The return of James IV of Scotland was expected for a hundred years or more after his death at Flodden Field in 1513, but it was from some remote and unspecified region and not, like that of Robert Bruce, from a Scottish hill or cave. When in 1578 Don Sebastian was defeated and killed in Morocco, the Portuguese refused to believe he was dead, in spite of the fact that a body alleged to be his was restored to them by the victorious Moors and duly buried in Belem. Shortly afterwards Spain, profiting by the failure of heirs to the Portuguese throne, annexed the country, and a tradition thereupon sprang up that Sebastian still lived and was reigning in the mysterious Island of the Seven Cities, whence he would return to free his country and drive out the hated Spaniards. In 1761 a monk was charged before the Inquisition with spreading false prophecies of his imminent coming and so undermining the already doubtful loyalty of the people to their alien masters. In 1825 an article in *The Times* described the old belief as still active at that time both in Portugal itself and in Brazil.

Sir Francis Drake's bodily death was not denied by anyone, but it was long believed without question that he would come back from Heaven if any summoned him by beating on his drum when England was in danger. Tradition says that as he lay dying he asked that the drum should be taken home and hung upon the wall, and promised that if this was done he would answer its call whenever he was needed. The legend altered in course of time and the emphasis shifted from the hero to the object. The drum itself acquired a magical significance, and is now believed to beat without human agency before a war. According to local tradition it was heard in 1914, and many sailors assert that it rolled again at Scapa Flow when the German ships were sunk there at the end of the Great War. In *The Phantom Ship* R. L. Hadfield quotes a curious story concerning a silver replica of the drum which was given to H.M.S. *Devonshire* in 1929. For some reason both officers and men conceived the idea that this replica of a magical object was unlucky, and several serious accidents, including the loss of seventeen lives through an explosion, were put down to its agency. So firm was the crew's belief in its uncanny powers that when the ship put to sea in 1936 it was decided to leave the silver drum behind, and it was accordingly hung in St. Nicholas's Church, Devonport. But though the drum has in some measure ousted its owner in popular tradition, Drake's promise was long remembered. In Devonshire until quite recently it was said that he had in fact returned to fight on several occasions, not in his own form, but in the bodies of other famous sailors, and that both Blake and Nelson were reincarnations of his spirit.

Even in our own day the age-old legend is not entirely dead. It reappears from time to time in the fragmentary form of a simple denial of the reported death, however strong the evidence for it may be, followed by an explanatory theory that the individual in question is no more seen, not because he is dead, but because he has gone on some secret journey for political or other reasons. Such theories cannot now survive the natural span of a life, for the old faith which could ignore the passage of centuries is lacking, but that they spring up as spontaneously in modern as in earlier times can hardly be denied by any who remember the loss of Lord Kitchener, or the many curious stories which followed the deaths of Sir Hector Macdonald and Adolf Hitler.

The undying hero appears in one form or another in almost every European country. In Switzerland the three founders of the Swiss Federation slept in the Grutli, near the spot where they first swore to free their people from foreign tyranny. Once a shepherd entered the cleft in the rock that contained them, and they roused themselves to ask the hour. The man replied that it was noon, whereupon the heroes said, "It is not yet time", and fell asleep once more. In Norway the expected deliverer was Olaf Tryggvason and in Sweden Olaf Redbeard, who opened his eyes every seven years and then returned to slumber. The German hero Siegfried slept in the Geroldseck; in Spain the defeated Moors once looked for the return of Alfatimi, who would come riding upon a green horse from the Sierra de Aguar and destroy all Spanish Christians. In the Balkans, Marko the shepherd was believed to lie in Urvina with his horse, Sharatz; when his sword rises out of the mountain-top and is seen by all he will waken and deliver his people.

Charles the Great slept in the Odenberg, once the abode of Woden, and also in the Unterberg, near Salzburg. In Upper Alsace a company of his soldiers lived in a huge underground camp from which they rode out once in every seven years. A local folk-tale tells of a baker's daughter who once met a soldier riding on a white horse down a lane near her home. He led her through a subterranean passage to a great cavern in which sat a host of men with flowing beards. To them she sold her bread, not only on that day but for several years thereafter, so that her father became very wealthy. One day she fell ill and sent her brother with the loaves, but he found the entrance to the passage blocked, and since that time no one has been able to enter the camp again.

These stragglers from Charles's conquering armies were not the future deliverers of Alsace, but blasphemers who, in an excess of pride, once dared to turn their arms against Heaven itself. The earth opened and swallowed them up, and thenceforward they were doomed to remain in their subterranean cavern, coming out only at seven-year intervals to exercise their horses. Probably they too were originally regarded as rescuing heroes until their splendid legend was partially forgotten and a more pious tinge was given to the old belief. That their story has suffered at least one modern change is shown by the fact that the weapons they used in their presumptuous assault were not swords or spears, as might have been expected, but guns and cannon. In Alsace also dwelt the hero Diedrich, his hand always on his sword-hilt and his gaze turned eastward, watching for the day when the Turks should water their horses in the Rhine, and he should ride out to drive them back whence they came.

Ogier the Dane, one of Charles the Great's famous Paladins, is claimed by both France and Denmark. In the latter country he lived in a vaulted chamber under the Castle of Kronberg, surrounded by his mail-clad followers. They slept with their heads upon a stone table, through the top of which Ogier's beard had grown; when they moved in their sleep their armour clashed and rattled and was sometimes heard on still nights by wayfarers passing the castle. Every seven years the hero stamped upon the floor with his iron mace. His hand-grasp left marks upon a bar of iron; when he lifted his head the stone table split from end to end, but his beard remained unharmed. In France he had no earthly resting-place, for Morgan le Fay caught him away to Avalon at the end of his long and adventurous life. There he remained for two hundred years, wearing a crown of myrtle and laurel which caused him to forget his past and all he had loved. But when France was attacked by Paynims her cries broke the enchantment and he returned to this world to save both her and Christendom. Then he went back to Avalon where, according to the old tradition, he still waits until France shall once more call upon him in the hour of supreme danger.

The saintly King Wenzel of Bohemia and his knights lived in the Blanik Mountain and rode out every night to exercise their horses on the plain. Here also was Ulrich von Rosenberg who fell at Litic, fighting against the hosts of Chichka. When he and his men presented themselves at the gates of Heaven, God ordered them to keep watch in the Blanik until they should be needed to defend Bohemia against another powerful foe. In the Carpathians the hero was less altruistic. He was Dobocz, the robber chief, who lived in a cave on the Czornahora and passed his time in counting his stolen gold. He was sometimes seen riding over the mountains, but no man willingly visited him in his cavern; those who entered it never returned to their homes but were seized by the robbers and forced to join their band. No one looked to Dobocz for deliverance or aid, but it was believed that when the appointed day came he would leave the mountain for the last time and revenge himself upon the people who betrayed him long ago.

The Seven Sleepers of Ephesus were more closely akin to those who are caught away to Fairyland or Paradise for a season than to the true undying hero. They slept only for a limited period, and after their death no second return was ever expected. Their bones, however, retained the power of prophecy and turned from one side to the other whenever danger threatened the city. Christian and Mohammedan versions of their story vary somewhat; the best known is that which Jacques de Voragine tells in *The Golden Legend*. According to this, the Sleepers were Christians who, during the Decian persecution in the third century, fled to a cavern on Mount Celion. Their hiding-place was discovered; the mouth of the cave was blocked with stones, and they were left to perish of cold and starvation. Three hundred and sixty years later, when Christianity was firmly established in the Empire, the cave-mouth was opened by a man who required stones with which to build a new stable. He found the seven martyrs peacefully sleeping within, as young as they had been when they first entered the cave and quite unharmed by three centuries of imprisonment. When roused from their enchanted sleep they at once asked what Decius intended to do with them; only with difficulty were they persuaded that more than one night had passed since they were walled into the cavern.

At that period of heresy denying the resurrection of the dead was raging in Ephesus, and this naturally gave added interest to the already remarkable story of the seven martyrs. They were closely questioned by the Bishop and by the Governor of the city and were then taken before the Emperor Theodosius. They declared that God had brought them back to the world to testify that the dead do indeed rise again, and then, having helped by their evidence to destroy the heresy, they bowed their heads and died. Theodosius wished to enshrine their remains in golden reliquaries, but they appeared to him in a dream and requested that their bodies should be allowed to rest for ever in the cave which had miraculously preserved them for so long.

This version of the story is clearly a Christian embroidery on an old legend which existed long before Christianity. The traditions of many races contain stories of people who visited Fairyland or the kingdom of the dead, and remained there for what seemed to be a few days, only to find on their return that hundreds of years had elapsed and all who had known them were dead. Like the Seven Sleepers, such people often died soon afterwards, but unlike them they had no message to deliver, and their sojourn in the supernatural region seems to have served no definite purpose. Such a legend may well have been told about Mount Celion before the time of Decius and have been inherited by martyrs in his reign, especially if, as is possible, any were buried there in his day. Nor is Ephesus the only locality connected with the Sleepers, for in Algeria they are said to have slept at N'gaous, and a cave in the Hirak Valley in Afghanistan was long known by their name.

In the Mohammedan version of the tale they slept only for one hundred years and, on waking, foretold the coming of the Prophet. They had with them a dog which also possessed the gift of prophecy and was one of the ten animals to be admitted to the Mohammedan Paradise. William of Malmesbury quotes a curious story concerning Edward the Confessor who, whilst dining at Westminster during the Easter festival, had a vision of the Seven Sleepers in their cavern and saw them turn from their right sides to their left. A deputation of learned men was sent from England to inquire into the truth of the matter. On arrival at Ephesus they were told by the citizens that the bodies had lain on their right sides for centuries and were certainly doing so still. When, however, they entered the cave they saw that all lay on the left, exactly as the King had described. The local people regarded this change as an exceedingly evil omen for their city, since the Sleepers were traditionally supposed to move only when sorrow and disaster threatened.

Europe's most famous sleeping hero was Frederick Barbarossa, who dwelt with his followers in the Kyffhauser, in Thuringia. The cavern in which he slept was brilliantly lit by magic and was adorned with gold and jewels and flowering trees. Down the centre ran a pure stream over sands of gold. The Emperor sat before a stone table round which his red beard had already grown twice; tradition said that when it had surrounded the table a third time he would waken and return to the world. He would hang his shield on a withered tree which would immediately break into leaf, and a better day would dawn for all mankind. On certain days of the year the mountain opened, and those who had the courage could enter and find their way down to the enchanted cavern. A shepherd once went in and played to the sleeping host on his pipe. The Emperor awoke and asked: "Fly the ravens round the mountain still?" On hearing that they did, he said he must sleep another hundred years. The shepherd was given a golden basin from the armoury; other visitors often received seemingly useless objects like handfuls of horse-meal or knots of flax, but these were always afterwards found to have turned into pure gold.

In many of the stories told of Frederick Barbarossa the gifts were dispensed by a maiden who acted as his housekeeper. Once a swineherd was invited to help himself from the treasures lying on the table. He filled his pockets and was about to leave when the housekeeper pointed to a flower which lay beside the jewels.

"Forget not the best," she said, but the man took no notice, and in due course he was punished. As he was leaving the mountain the great doors slammed upon his heel and injured him so seriously that he died in agony. On another occasion a party of musicians returning from a feast stopped outside the gates to play a tune for the old Emperor. A woman came out of the hill and rewarded them with horses' heads, which all but one man threw away as worthless. In the morning the remaining head was found to be a solid lump of gold.

In these tales the human leader is definitely linked with the gods, for the housekeeper is Dame Holle, one of the ancient Teutonic goddesses. Her connexion with the locality is undoubtedly older than that of the Emperor, and the holy character of the mountain probably accounts for the fact that he was expected to return from there, and not from Asia Minor, where he was drowned in 1190. In many of these mountain legends the choice of a resting-place for a particular hero seems to have been dictated less by his own connexion with it than by the fact that the mountain or cave was already regarded as sacred. The dwelling of some god or nature-spirit became the dwelling of the dead leader who gradually took on the attributes of his predecessor and usurped his place. Charles the Great succeeded Woden in the Odenberg; the mysterious riders who issued nightly from the Donnersberg were clearly Thor's followers once, though the god had been forgotten and only his band remembered. The treasure-guarding Knights Templars who sat gambling in the Rollberg may once have been trolls or mountain-spirits, whose presence sanctified the district centuries before the persecution of the Templars made them objects of superstitious horror or unavailing pity to their contemporaries. Not infrequently, when a hill or cave had long been associated with the kingdom of the dead, the hero connected with it became confused with the ancient ruler of that kingdom and, like Arthur in Mount Etna, had power to summon those about to die.

That the place was often more important than its traditional human inhabitant is shown by the fact that some mountains contained more than one hero. The Blanik, as we have seen, housed both King Wenzel and Ulrich von Rosenberg. A third story claimed that it was not either of these but the Knight Stoymir who lived within it and nightly watered his horses in a nearby stream. Frederick Barbarossa was sometimes confused with the Emperor Otto and with the Marquis John, both of whom were said to sleep in the Kyffhauser. The Marquis had none of the friendliness of the old Emperor. He sat with his long nails growing into the table, surrounded by wine-vats so ancient that their wood and hoops had rotted away; the wine within them had formed its own shell and stood up of itself. A wine-glass with a few dregs left in the bottom stood before him on the table. Once a joiner entered the chamber and drank from the glass, with the result that he fell asleep and did not wake for seven years. In the Eildon Hills the sleeper was variously called King Arthur or Thomas the Rhymer, the thirteenth-century prophet having apparently taken the place of the sixth-century warrior in a district always closely associated with the supernatural.

Moreover, in some places the in-dweller was unidentified, and only a vague tradition alleged that some great person lay within the cave or mountain, waiting for the day when he should manifest himself. That such unexplained individuals must once have been local nature-spirits, only later confused with hero-myths, can hardly be doubted. The Guckenberg contained an unnamed Emperor and his host who, many centuries before, had disappeared within after some forgotten battle, leaving no story behind them but the tradition of their presence. In West Gothland a cleft known as the Giant's Path was supposed to lead to a subterranean chamber where a solitary man lay sleeping on a stone. His name and story were alike unknown, but it was believed that he was enchanted until Doomsday, and that whenever the bell tolled in Yglunda Church he turned in his sleep and sighed. The Devil's Den in the Isle of Man was once thought to lead into a hidden hall in which dwelt a great prince of unknown lineage who had never died, but who was bound by spells for six hundred years. A Sutherlandshire folk-tale relates how a man once strayed into a vast cave filled with men of gigantic stature who rested upon their elbows on the floor. A bugle lay on the table in the centre of the chamber. The man picked it up and blew upon it twice; at the first note all stirred, at the second the leader of the company said, "Do not do that again or you will wake us." The intruder fled, and from that day to this no one has ever been able to find the cave again.

Of the known sleeping-heroes of Britain, the most famous was, of course, Arthur, of whom more must be said later. He slept in several places, sometimes alone, but more usually with his knights and followers. His legend was preserved and embroidered not only by the Britons whom he once led, but also by the English, against whose ancestors he waged his desperate wars, and by the Normans whose poets turned him into the typical King of the Age of Chivalry. Belief in his continued existence persisted in some districts down to the end of the nineteenth century, and innumerable place-names up and down the country still show how strong was his hold upon the imagination of the people. But if he was the most celebrated, he was not the only British hero whose death was passionately denied when it occurred, and whose re-appearance was expected for periods varying from a few years to several centuries. In some cases the tradition faded quickly and amounted to little more than a series of rumours based on an instinctive refusal to credit evil tidings. Harold's death at Hastings was at first denied by the defeated English. It was said he had been rescued from the battle-field and secretly nursed back to health in Winchester, whence he escaped to the Continent to seek aid from the kings of Europe. A later legend says that when all had refused him, he came back to England in disguise and ended his days as a hermit near St. John's Church in Chester, unknown to all until he revealed his identity on his death-bed.

Richard II's death in 1399 was similarly disbelieved. After his abdication he was taken to Pontefract Castle as a prisoner and was never seen again. There can be little doubt that he was murdered there, but many people believed that he had escaped and was in Scotland. To allay these rumours Henry IV brought his body to London and exposed it for all to see in St. Paul's Cathedral. Even this did not shake his supporters' faith in his continued existence. It was said that the body was not his, but that of his chaplain, who closely resembled him. Owen Glendower, when he raised his standard of revolt in 1400, declared that Richard was alive in Scotland, and for some time a man claiming to be the dead King was entertained at the Scottish court by Robert. In 1403 a rumour spread through Cheshire that Richard was hiding at Sandiway, waiting to join the Percies in their rebellion, and belief in this rumour was one of the reasons why the Cheshire men, who had loved him, rallied so enthusiastically to that ill-fated cause. But these tales, like those concerning Harold, were short-lived and had not the strength to withstand the cold logic of facts; the strong and the weak king alike belong to the history of our land, but never attained a permanent place in its folk-lore.

Other heroes have died and been buried with their fathers without any expectation of their return, but have continued to watch over the destinies of their country and, by ghostly appearances, to warn her of coming disasters. The Black Prince was, and still is, supposed to haunt Hall Place, in Kent, where he stayed on his way to the French wars, and to appear there before any British defeat. It is recorded that he was seen three times during the Great War, and always before a military reverse. Another and far less likely spirit returned when any serious misfortune threatened either the nation as a whole or a member of the royal family. This was Herne the Hunter, the sinister forest warden who, in Henry VIII's reign, practised witchcraft under an oak in Windsor Great Park and subsequently hanged himself upon it. He, too, has been seen in modern times, notably before the trade depression of 1931. Nothing in his life, so far as we know it, suggested ardent patriotism or concern for others, and there seems to be no obvious reason why he should be supposed to interest himself in England's welfare after his death. But the nature of his appearances may provide a clue. He appeared near the place where the oak formerly grew, wearing horns upon his head and sometimes accompanied by a hart which issued from a hollow anciently associated with fairies. He had been feared for his sorceries in life, and it seems probable that in later years his ghost was confused with some far older spirit of ominous character, who once dwelt in or near the oak and whose connexion with the tree may explain Herne's choice of that spot for his unhallowed rites.

Wild Edric rode out from the lead mines of Shropshire whenever England was faced with war, but in this case it was not a ghost that was seen but the man himself. Across the border, in Wales, slept Merlin in a cave near Carmarthen which is known by his name, and which is usually said to be the place where Vivian bound him by her treacherous spell. In Wales also slept Owen Lawgoch and the more famous Owen Glendower. Of the former, little is known except that he was one of the last chieftains to fall in battle against the English invaders. He slept with his men on Mynnydd Mawr, near Llandilo, waiting for the day when a trumpet note and the clash of arms on Rhywgoch should rouse him to fight again, this time victoriously.

Owen Glendower died a natural death in 1415 in his daughter's house at Monnington Straddel. An uninscribed stone in the churchyard of Monnington-on-Wye was once supposed to mark his grave, but this tradition can only have sprung from a confusion between two places of similar name. Monnington Straddel was Alice Scudamore's home, and there her father died; it is hardly likely that his body should have been carried across country to rest in an unnamed grave at a place with which he had no particular connexion and which was, at that time, in the hands of his enemies. But wherever his actual tomb may have been, Welsh loyalty and devotion were too strong for the simple facts of the case to be readily accepted. He was their leader by right of courage, of magical knowledge, and of royal descent, for he claimed to be descended from Prince Llewellyn on his mother's side. His rising in 1400 was supported by all ardent patriots, and when, later, he was forced to take to the mountains and live in hiding, his people shielded him and helped him by every means in their power. To the end of his life he harassed the English by repeated and daring raids from Craig-y-Dorth and other hiding-places and, unlike Wild Edric, he never made peace with his enemies. Henry V offered to pardon him, and it is possible that he might have accepted this grace in the end, but, perhaps fortunately for his reputation, he died before the negotiations were completed. Henceforth he was said to sleep in Castle Cave in the Vale of Gwent, until England shall become degenerate through her own vices, and he can once more assert the independence of Wales, never to be questioned again until the Day of Judgment.

James IV of Scotland lived on as an undying hero for about a hundred years after his death, but the legend of the earlier Robert Bruce was much more persistent. He lay with his men on Rathlin Island, under a ruin known as Bruce's Castle. The entrance to this cave was usually invisible, but at seven-year intervals it opened upon the outer world, and the mail-clad warriors could be seen sleeping round their chief, with a half-sheathed sabre before them. Tradition said that when Bruce finally returned, the island would be united to the rest of Scotland and the old king would begin a second and more peaceful reign. In Ireland Brian Boru was once looked for to drive out the English, but in later times his place was taken by Earl Gerald, who slept under the Rath of Mullaghmast. Every seven years he rode round the Curragh of Kildare on a horse whose shoes were of silver. When he was first enchanted these shoes were half an inch thick; when they are worn as thin as a cat's ear the spell will be broken by a trumpet sounded by a miller's son with six fingers on each hand. Then the sorcerer Earl and his men will leave the Rath for the last time and finally defeat the English, after which he will reign for forty years as King of a united Ireland.

In modern times the old instinctive belief has reappeared occasionally in the form of a crop of rumours following upon the death or disappearance of some great man. Napoleon Bonaparte seems an unlikely hero for any but the French to hope for, but in his *Lipovenismulu* Bishop Melchisedech of Roumania refers to a Slavonic sect which revered him, and maintained that he had not died at St. Helena, but was living at Irkousk, whence he would return at the head of a powerful army and once more conquer the world. The Bulgarian peasantry expected the return of Prince Alexander for some time after he died in exile, in spite of the fact that he had abdicated in 1886, supposedly of his own free will. But the circumstances preceding that abdication, and particularly the incident of his kidnapping and forcible removal to Reni, had implanted a deep suspicion in the minds of the people which, in an earlier age, would almost certainly have caused him to be regarded as an undying hero, and nearly did so then. The great and unquestioning trust which almost everyone reposed in Lord Kitchener at the beginning of World War I made his tragic death in 1916 appear an irreparable disaster. As soon as the news was known, rumours began to circulate that he was still alive and had been sent on a mission so secret that the Government had spread the story of his death to deceive the enemy. Alternatively, he was said to be a prisoner, either in Russia or elsewhere. Not for some time was it generally admitted that the man who, by his strong personality and gifts of leadership, had succeeded in raising the great armies of the time from an unmilitary nation would never return to lead his country again.

Perhaps the most curious recrudescence of the ancient legend is seen in the stories concerning Sir Hector Macdonald. He was the son of a Ross-shire crofter who rose to fame and high position in the Army. He distinguished himself everywhere by his courage and initiative and was immensely popular, not only with his own men, but with all Highlanders. Nearly every homestead contained his photograph, and his name was a household word throughout the north of Scotland. In 1903 he committed suicide in Paris, as the result of some trouble in which he had become involved whilst commanding the British forces in Ceylon and which so preyed on his mind that its balance was temporarily shaken. His body was taken back to Scotland, where the Highland societies proposed to give him a magnificent funeral, with all the honours which they could bestow. For some reason, however, he was buried very quietly in Edinburgh at six o'clock in the morning, without military rites of any kind and without even a flag upon his coffin. This curious secrecy at once raised suspicion, and so infuriated the people that the police were obliged to guard the grave for a month after the funeral. Rumours began to spread that he was not dead at all, and when the Russo-Japanese war broke out, eleven months later, it was said in many districts that he was fighting on the Russian side.

So strong was the belief in his continued existence that subscriptions came in only very slowly for the great monument to his memory which now stands on Mitchell Hill at Dingwall. The people who had admired him most would not contribute to a memorial for a man whom they believed to be still living. In the Great War two separate and opposing stories were told of him. He was said to be fighting for the Allies in Russia, and one of the principal reasons for Lord Kitchener's fatal journey to that country was supposed to be a desire to see him. On the other hand, he was alleged to be fighting on the German side. General von Mackensen was believed to be Hector Macdonald in disguise, and in support of this theory it was asserted that this General never fought against English or Scottish troops in any of his battles.

More than forty years later the old legend reared its head once more, though only for a brief space. When Adolf Hitler died in 1945, his death was followed by a crop of rumours. He was not dead, it was said, but somewhere in hiding, and he would emerge again to lead and inspire his people. Strong measures had to be taken by the Allies to crush this belief which, if unchecked, might have developed into a dangerous political force. Modern conditions do not encourage the persistence of legends which have no foundation in fact, and this new myth died away quickly. But for a moment the old pattern of thought was clearly visible; and Hitler surprisingly appeared as the unworthy successor of those splendid heroes who from time to time have adorned this universal and age-old story.

AVALON

CHAPTER III

KING ARTHUR

HARDLY anything is known to us of the real life and
history of the man whom we now call King Arthur. We
do not know where he was born, or in what district he
was brought up. Cornish tradition gives him a kingly father and
Tintagel as a birthplace, and it seems probable that he had his
beginnings somewhere in the West. He may have been the son
of a British chieftain, or of some well-established Roman family
which remained in Britain after the withdrawal of the legions. His
rank and parentage are alike obscure, though the former must have
been sufficiently distinguished to give him a voice in his country's
councils. Even the date of his death has been variously calculated,
and his grave is still undiscovered. He appears suddenly before us
as an able and vigorous military leader in one of the darkest periods
of our history, when the Saxon conquest was not yet complete and
all that remained of the old Romano-British civilization was struggling desperately against successive waves of pagan invasion. We
are told that he was the commander of the British forces and that
he won for his countrymen a much-needed breathing space in a
series of twelve battles, all of them in places which cannot now
be identified. After the greatest of these victories—that of Mount

Badon—there was peace for twenty-one years, and then his work was destroyed by dissensions amongst the Britons themselves. Arthur fell at the Battle of Camlann; presumably he was buried, but no one knows where. Later tradition insisted that he did not die, but was magically transported to Avalon, or to some other resting-place, to return, like other sleeping heroes, when his country should need him most.

Only two early historians mention him by name—Nennius, who wrote early in the ninth century, and the compiler of the *Annales Cambriae*, whose entries end with the year 977. Gildas, who was born in the year of Mount Badon and whose boyhood therefore coincided with Arthur's last years, does not refer to him at all. In his impassioned account of the distresses of Britain he speaks only of Ambrosius Aurelianus, who seems to have been Arthur's immediate predecessor in the British leadership. He refers to the Battle of Mount Badon without naming the general who won it, and in his bitter diatribes against his countrymen, to whose sins he attributes all their misfortunes, only Ambrosius is praised. The *Anglo-Saxon Chronicle* ignores both the British leaders, and the Venerable Bede, who relied upon Gildas for this early period, merely repeats what he learnt from that bigoted chronicler. Yet in spite of these scanty historical references the fame of Arthur persisted in folk-tale and legend, and has been preserved to us for fourteen hundred years, at first by tradition and bardic songs, and later by the romantic writings of the Middle Ages, which glorified his career and transformed a simple patriot leader of the sixth century into a mighty king, the type and example of all that a Christian knight of the Age of Chivalry should be.

The fantastic stories that gathered round his name for long obscured his probable historicity and made him appear a shadowy folk-lore figure who existed only in the imagination of a backward-looking people. Yet these tales of magical powers and fairy connexions, of giant-like attributes and kingly virtues, and, above all, of a looked-for return after death, are precisely the stories that most usually gather round the memory of a victorious leader, now dead, but remembered with passion and longing by the oppressed people for whom he fought. They cannot be taken as proof that their central figure is mythical, for some of them, as we have seen,

39

have been told about such undoubtedly genuine individuals as Wild Edric, Robert Bruce and Sir Francis Drake. Historical probability is on the side of a real Arthur. Gildas cannot have been incorrect about the Battle of Mount Badon and the events immediately following, for they occurred in his own lifetime. Though he does not mention Arthur in this connexion, persistent tradition does, and it would be natural for the hero who won so important a victory to be remembered and praised, with ever-growing accretions of the marvellous, for long afterwards. Folk-memory is not always trustworthy in detail, but few tenacious traditions are entirely without foundation. A victory sufficiently decisive to secure twenty years of peace would make a great impression, and the name of the leader concerned would be handed down for generations afterwards. The general concensus of modern opinion is that Arthur did, in fact, exist, that he fought the Saxons successfully at some period between A.D. 503 and A.D. 520, that his victories were followed by a long interlude of calm, and that he died in battle at a date variously given as A.D. 537, 539 and 542.

There is no real evidence that he was a king, and certainly none that he was King of all Britain. Nennius says he fought with the kings of the Britons and was their leader in war, but he does not say that he was himself royal. It seems probable that he was the unanimously chosen commander-in-chief of a mixed British force which fought wherever it was most needed and co-operated with the local levies in the threatened districts. In the later years of Roman rule the *comes Britanniarum* commanded a mobile army capable of being used in any part of the country, and it has been suggested that Arthur held a position analogous to that of the old Counts of Britain. Such a position would give him a power and influence more widespread than that of any local king, or even the temporary head of a defensive confederation of such kings, and may account for the fact that traditions concerning him are found in such widely separated parts of the island as Scotland, Cornwall, Yorkshire, Wales, Somerset and Cheshire.

The period in which he lived was sufficiently troubled to call forth all that was heroic in any leader. The withdrawal of the Roman garrison in the early part of the fifth century had left a Romanized and mostly Christian Britain exposed to intermittent attacks by Picts and Scots from the north and by Saxons from overseas. Such raids, though harassing and dangerous, did not immediately disorganize the ordinary life of the people or destroy their inherited Roman culture. Gildas tells us that after the first period of confusion and a fruitless appeal to Rome for help, the Britons rallied and repulsed the Picts, and that afterwards "the island overflowed with such an abundant supply as is remembered in no former age, whereupon luxury increased in every way."[1] The biographer of St. Germanus speaks of Britain as "that most wealthy island",[2] and his account of the saint's visit in A.D. 429 shows that he found a people still Christian and civilized, following their ancient way of life in spite of the perils of the time, and able to defend themselves more or less successfully against sporadic raids. St. Germanus himself led a British force against a mixed army of Picts and Saxons, and defeated them without bloodshed in the famous Hallelujah victory. He was able to make gifts to a yet undevastated shrine of St. Alban the Martyr and to return to Gaul without misadventure, over a sea apparently still safe for travellers.

It was not until the middle of the century that serious Saxon invasions, followed by permanent settlement on conquered British lands, began in earnest. King Vortigern is blamed by the early chroniclers for allowing the enemy to gain their first foothold, but what he did was probably only a hastening of the inevitable. Driven by the double fear of renewed invasion by the Picts and Scots and of attack by Ambrosius Aurelianus, with whom he seems to have been at enmity, he called in the aid of a Saxon mercenary force which, with the help of reinforcements from overseas, established itself firmly in Kent and eventually turned on the country it had come to protect. The *Anglo-Saxon Chronicle* says briefly:

> . . . Hengest and Horsa, invited by Wyrtgeorn, sought Britain, in the place which is named *Ypwines fleot* (Ebbsfleet), at first as a help to the Britons, but later they fought against them.

Gildas gives us more details. He describes how Vortigern called a council meeting, and how:

> . . . all the councillors, together with their haughty king, are so blinded that (devising a help, say rather a destruction for the country)

---

[1] Gildas: *Liber de Excidio et Conquestu Britanniae.*
[2] Constantius of Lyons, *Life of St. Germanus.* c. 480.

they introduced those ferocious Saxons of unspeakable name, hateful to God and men, bringing as it were wolves unto the fold in order to beat back the nations of the North. . . . A flock of cubs burst forth from the lair of the barbaric lioness in three keels as they call them in their language, that is in three warships, with a favourable wind and with good augury. For it had been foretold them, by a prophecy on which they relied, that for 300 years they would hold the country to which they were directing their prows, and that for half that time, that is 150 years, they would often lay it waste. By the order of that luckless king they landed first in the eastern part of the island, and there fixed their horrible claws, pretending that they were going to fight for our country, but really to fight against it. Their motherland, learning of the success of her first band, sends forth a larger body of these mercenary dogs, which come across in ships, and is united with the bastard men-at-arms already here. From that time the seed of iniquity, the root of bitterness, the poisonous growth worthy of our merits, springs up among us with shoots and tendrils of ferocity.[1]

He goes on to relate how the reinforced band sought opportunities of quarrel over the question of supplies, and how "a fire of just vengeance by reason of our former sins" spread over the country. He describes the sacking of cities, the devastation of the countryside, the murder of priests and people. He tells us that:

Terrible it was to see, in the midst of the streets, tops of towers torn from their lofty fittings, the stones of high walls, holy altars, fragments of bodies, covered with clotted blood, so that they seemed as if squeezed together in some ghastly wine press. There was no burial for the dead, save in the ruins of their homes, or the bellies of beasts and birds (with all reverence to the blessed souls, if indeed many such were found, which at that time were carried by the holy angels to Heaven). . . . Some of the wretched remnant were caught in the mountains and all murdered there; others, forced by famine, surrendered, to be for ever the slaves of their foes, if indeed they were not slain on the spot— verily the greatest favour; others with great wailing sought the regions beyond the sea. . . .[2]

A few, more hardy or more fortunate, hid in the hills and forests and survived to form the nucleus of the army raised by Ambrosius Aurelianus. With the appearance of this "modest man, who alone

---

[1] Gildas, op. cit.   [2] Gildas, op. cit.

of the Roman nation was left alive amid the tumult of so troubled a time", the tide of disaster was stemmed. From that time onwards sometimes the Britons and sometimes the Saxons were victorious until the year of Mount Badon, a battle which Gildas describes as "almost the last slaughter of these gallows-birds, but by no means the least." He does not tell us the name of the commander, but he says that afterwards the war ceased and, because they were mindful of past horrors and their merciful deliverance from them, "kings, public magistrates, private persons, priests and ecclesiastics all did their duty" until the rise of a new generation that had not known the war brought with it a renewal of civil strife and of evil rulers.

In all this there is no word of Arthur, unless we may assume that he is included amongst the virtuous kings and magistrates of the peace period. Possibly Gildas considered that anything which happened in the lifetime of his father and grandfather was too recent and well known to need very careful recording. In any case, he was not an historian in the modern sense, but a religious bigot who was more concerned to denounce those whom he considered to be evildoers than to record in detail the events of his age. Beyond the bare mention of Mount Badon and its consequences, he tells us very little of what happened after the rise of Ambrosius Aurelianus, and his book ends in bitter denunciation of five living kings, who had earned his rather facile disapproval.

Nennius, however, states definitely that Arthur was the victor of Mount Badon. He is also our sole authority for the names of the other eleven battles in the campaign. In his *Historia Brittonum* he refers to Arthur without preamble or explanation, as though all his readers would be already familiar with his name. In another section of the book—that dealing with the wonders of Britain—he speaks of Anir as the son of "the warrior Arthur" which, presumably, was identification enough in the ninth century. These "wonders" show that legend and myth were already busy with the dead leader's memory. We hear of a cairn at Buelt, where Arthur's dog, Cabal, had left his footprint on hard stone, and of the miraculous grave of his son Anir at Ercing, which constantly changed its length, no matter how many times and how carefully it was measured. But this folk-lore section is quite distinct from the straightforward story of the struggle between Britons and Saxons, in which Nennius says:

> When Hengest was dead, Octha his son crossed from the north part of Britain to the kingdom of Kent. From him the kings of Kent spring. Then Arthur fought against them in those days, with the kings of the Britons, but he was their leader in war. The first battle was at the mouth of the river Glein. The second, and the third, and the fourth, and the fifth on another river called Dubglas, in the land Linnuis. The sixth, on the river called Bassas. The seventh in the wood Celidon, that is *Cat Coit Celidon* (the battle of the wood Celidon). The eighth was the battle in Castle Guinnion, in which Arthur carried on his shoulders the representation of the Blessed Virgin Mary, and the heathen were turned to flight in that day, and great was the slaughter of them, through the virtue of our Lord Jesus Christ and His mother, the Blessed Virgin Mary. The ninth battle was in the City of the Legion. He fought his tenth battle on the shore of the river called Tribuit. The eleventh battle was in the mountain called Agned. The twelfth battle was on Mount Badon, in which there fell in one day 960 men from the onslaught of Arthur only, and no one laid them low, save he alone. And in all his battles he was the victor.

Here we have Arthur fully fledged, a Christian patriot leader defending his country against pagan invaders, defeating them by his superior generalship, and apparently fighting the last battle with a force of his own raising, unassisted by that of any allied king. Much ink has been expended upon the identification of the battle-fields, but in spite of many varying suggestions they remain uncertain. It seems probable that Mount Badon was somewhere in south-western or western England, though Mr. Stuart Glennie in *Arthurian Localities* puts the whole campaign in Scotland and Northumberland. To Nennius, who tells us that he drew his facts from earlier writings known to him and who must have been helped by strong living tradition, they were doubtless known places, needing no further identification from him. Gildas also takes it for granted that his readers know where Mount Badon —the only battle he mentions by name—was situated.

The dates as well as the places are obscure. Gildas says that Mount Badon, the last of the campaign, was fought in "the forty-fourth year, as I know, with one month elapsed, which is also the year of my birth." What he meant by this is much disputed, but if, as some scholars have thought, he meant forty-four years after the first victories of Ambrosius Aurelianus, this reckoning would agree with the relevant entry in the *Annales Cambriae*; it would also support the suggestion that Arthur succeeded Ambrosius Aurelianus as the British leader, either because the latter was dead, or because he was too old to continue the fight. The date given by the *Annales* is A.D. 516; the entry says that "Arthur carried the cross of our Lord Jesus Christ for three days and three nights on his shoulders, and the Britons were the victors." The compiler of this Welsh chronicle carries the story a step farther. Twenty-one years later, under the year A.D. 537, he records: "The Battle of Camlann, in which Arthur and Medraut fell." This is the first mention of the man who is more generally known as Modred and whom Geoffrey of Monmouth asserts was the son of Arthur's sister, Anna.

In 1125 we hear of Arthur again in the pages of another historian. William of Malmesbury, in his *Gesta Regum*, describes Ambrosius Aurelianus as king of the Britons, and Arthur as his contemporary and the general of his armies. His account is interesting to us now, not so much for the record of Arthur's life as for the reference to a cloud of legends which had grown up round his name, and which were actively believed by many in the twelfth century. To William such legends were mere nonsense, but he does not allow them to affect his own belief in Arthur as a person, once actually living and worthy of admiration. He says:

> On the death of Vortimer, the strength of the Britons grew faint, their diminished hopes went backwards; and straightway they would have come to ruin, had not Ambrosius, the sole survivor of the Romans, who was monarch of the realm after Vortigern, repressed the overweening barbarians through the distinguished achievements of the warlike Arthur. This is that Arthur of whom the trifling of the Britons talk such nonsense even to-day; a man clearly worthy not to be dreamed of in fallacious fables, but to be proclaimed in veracious histories as one who long sustained his tottering country, and gave the shattered minds of his fellow-citizens an edge for war. Finally, at the siege of Mount Badon, relying upon the image of the mother of the Lord, which he had sewn upon his armour, he made head single-handed against nine hundred of the enemy and routed them with incredible slaughter.

A few years after the appearance of *Gesta Regum*, at some period between 1135 and 1139, Geoffrey of Monmouth produced his *Historia Regum Britanniae*, which covered the supposed history of Britain from the time of Brutus to that of Cadwallader in the seventh century. This is a very different type of book from *Gesta Regum*, which was the work of a serious historian. It is a curious mixture of chronicle, fable and romance, in which the author uses his fertile imagination to embellish and adorn his material and to glorify the kings of Britain, especially Arthur. In spite of its manifest errors it has done more to mould our conception of Arthur than any other book, and every subsequent writer on the subject has drawn upon it, from Wace and Layamon down to Lord Tennyson. It first appeared in a romance-loving age and became immediately popular, though, even at that time, some doubt was thrown upon it, and especially upon its supposed source. Geoffrey asserted that he drew his facts, not only from the known histories of Bede and Gildas and from popular tales and bardic writings, but also, and principally, from an ancient book in the British tongue known only to himself and Walter, Archdeacon of Oxford, who brought it from Brittany. No one knows what book this is, or whether it had any actual existence outside the imagination of the chronicler. No trace of it has ever since been found, and Geoffrey never showed it to any of his critics in proof of his questioned veracity. This does not, of course, prove that there was no such book, but the mystery which surrounded it is at least suspicious. Geoffrey himself spoke of it as his chief source, and went so far as to warn other historians not to write about the early British kings, since they had not in their possession this all-important volume which set forth the doings of those kings "in stories of exceeding beauty."

The Arthurian section of the *Historia* makes Arthur a king, the son of Uther Pendragon and Igerne, wife of Gorlois, Duke of Cornwall. Magic enters at once into the tale, for Uther Pendragon is able, through Merlin's enchantments, to enter Tintagel Castle, where Igerne had been placed for safety in the likeness of her husband. Thus is Arthur conceived. At the age of fifteen he is crowned by St. Dubricius, and immediately begins his career of conquest. He first defeats the Saxons, and then turns his attention

Arthur: Hero of Romance and Chivalry

to wider fields, conquering Gaul and Ireland, Norway, Iceland and the Orkneys. He marries Guinevere, the daughter of a noble Roman family, and it is partly to please her that he embarks upon these foreign campaigns. His knights include such famous men as Kay and Bedevere, Gawain and Modred, and many others, all of whom are proud to wear his colours. His court is modelled on twelfth-century lines, and here he receives the vassal kings from the conquered territories. At Caerleon, his chief city, a college of two hundred philosophers, learned in astronomy, foretell by the stars the wonders of his reign. Knights from all parts vie with each other to be included in his following; the chaste and beautiful ladies of his court inspire them to greater feats of daring by refusing the love of any knight who has not thrice proved himself in the wars. Britain at this time surpasses all other kingdoms, not only in riches, but also "in the courteous wit of them that dwelt therein."

In the course of his adventures Arthur kills two giants, one of whom has a cloak made from the beards of fallen kings. At Mount Badon he bears a charmed shield and with his sword Caliburn kills 470 Saxons single-handed. The Romans having been so foolish as to challenge him, he makes war upon them in Gaul, slays their leader and sends his body to the Senate, and is just about to march on Rome itself when Modred's treachery recalls him to Britain. Here, after several battles, he defeats and kills Modred in the year A.D. 542 on the banks of the Camel, and is himself fatally wounded. Geoffrey does not commit himself, either to the statement that the King is dead, like other men, or to the belief that he will come again. He says, rather ambiguously, that he "was wounded to the death, and being born hence for the healing of his wounds to the island of Avallon, resigned the diadem of Britain to his kinsman, Constantine."

Here the account of Arthur ends. We are left with the picture of a powerful and virtuous king, a mighty warrior and a wise ruler, whose birth and death are faintly blurred with magic, and over whose court shines the bright light of romance and beauty. The chivalrous and courtly notions of Geoffrey's own time pervade the whole story; the witty, cultured ladies, the heroic knights, and even Caerleon, with its thronging ships and kingly palaces, are much more at home in the twelfth century than the sixth. The British leader, waging his desperate warfare against a merciless enemy or enjoying the subsequent period of peace amid the simple surroundings of his time, bears little resemblance to the magnificent king who henceforth is Arthur.

William of Malmesbury is the last writer who presents him, however slightly, as he must have been. From Geoffrey's time onwards poets and story-tellers busy themselves with his fame, making him always more mediaeval and more mystical, until his original character became completely overlaid. In their search for picturesque detail such writers as Wace, Marie de France, Layamon, Chretien de Troyes and Malory made use of old traditions and ballads, whether these had originally been told or sung about Arthur or not. The legend of the Holy Grail, for instance, had nothing whatever to do with Arthur in its original form, and some scholars maintain that the Round Table is really a very early Celtic institution dating from long before his time. With these embroideries we need not concern ourselves. What is more interesting is the persistent reappearance of the sleeping hero legend for which, had they so wished, these writers could have given the authority of many ancient traditions and the still active beliefs of their own day.

For that the belief existed in the twelfth and later centuries there is no doubt whatever. Alain de Lille says that it was not safe in Brittany to assert in any public place that Arthur was dead. "Hardly," he says, "will you escape unscathed without being whelmed by the curses or crushed by the stones of your hearers."[1] Nor was it any less dangerous in Cornwall. In 1113 the canons of Laon Cathedral visited Bodmin in the course of a pilgrimage to raise funds for the rebuilding of their city, burnt in an insurrection in the previous year. They brought with them the miracle-working shrine of Our Lady, at which many cures had already been wrought in various English towns and cities. A man with a withered hand came to be healed at Bodmin and, while he was keeping vigil in the church, he told one of the canons' followers that Arthur still lived. The Frenchman was foolish enough to scoff at his belief, and the result was a serious riot, during which

---

[1] *Prophetia Anglicana* (*c.* 1167–84).

armed and infuriated Cornishmen rushed into the church, and bloodshed was only narrowly averted by the strenuous efforts of the clerk Algardus, afterwards Bishop of Coutances.

This passionate belief in Arthur's return was strengthened by the fact that his grave had never been definitely located. William of Malmesbury says that Gawain's grave was found in Wales in the reign of William I, "but the tomb of Arthur was nowhere beheld, whence ancient ditties fable that he is yet to come". The *Black Book of Carmarthen*, one of the Four Ancient Books of Wales, gives a list of famous burial-places, but Arthur's is not among them:

> Osvran's sons' grave at Camlan,
> After many a slaughter,
> Bedwyr's grave in Allt Tryvan.
> A grave for March, a grave for Gwythur,
> A grave for Gwgawn of the ruddy sword.
> Not wise (the thought) a grave for Arthur.

In popular belief the thought was indeed not wise, for Arthur needed no tomb because he was not dead, and would return at the appointed time from whatever Celtic Paradise or underworld contained him. Even the alleged discovery of his bones at Glastonbury in 1190 or 1191 did little to shake this belief, and centuries afterwards he was still thought of as sleeping in hills or caves until the day of deliverance.

The story of that discovery is curious. The monks of Glastonbury claimed that his grave had been found between two ancient stone pyramids, bearing illegible inscriptions, which stood in their burial ground, near the old church. It is not quite clear whether the discovery was made by accident, or as a result of deliberate search. Ralph de Coggeshall says the bones were found when a grave was being dug for a monk who had expressed a desire to lie between the pyramids. Giraldus Cambrensis says that search was made for them on the advice of Henry II, who had learnt from an old British poet that they lay in a hollowed oak, sixteen feet or more below the surface of the burial ground. Here they had been secretly laid, without the pomp that was their due, for fear of the Saxons. The monks also possessed certain writings which suggested that the grave might be there, and some of them had seen it in visions and dreams. Adam de Domerham, the official historian of the Abbey, speaks as though the situation of the grave was already known, and says the exhumation took place because the Abbot had been "frequently admonished concerning the more honourable placing of the famous King Arthur." But Adam wrote a hundred years after the event and, though he had access to the Abbey records, his evidence is perhaps not so valuable as that of Giraldus, who was alive at the time.

The finding of the grave, whether accidental or otherwise, came at a most fortunate moment for the Abbey. A series of misfortunes had overtaken it in the preceding years, affecting both its prestige and its financial position. In 1184 a disastrous fire destroyed all the monastery buildings, and with them the oldest and most sacred church in the country. This was the wattle chapel of Our Lady, known as the Old Church, which many believed to have been built by men who had actually known Our Lord. Tradition said that when St. Phillip the Apostle was preaching in Gaul, he sent a band of twelve missionaries to Britain under the leadership of St. Joseph of Arimathea. These men came to Glastonbury and were given land by the pagan king of the district. Here St. Joseph planted the Holy Thorn, and here they built a chapel at the bidding of the Archangel Gabriel, just thirty-one years after the Crucifixion.

William of Malmesbury, who is our principal authority on the early history of Glastonbury, does not mention Joseph of Arimathea in his *De Antiquitate Glastoniensis Ecclesiae*, or at least, he does not in those parts of the book which were certainly written by him. In a thirteenth-century copy, now in Trinity College, Cambridge, an introductory chapter in another hand gives the full story, but this is believed to be a later addition. William believed the Old Church to have been built in A.D. 166 by missionaries sent to Britain at the request of King Lucius. He refers only cautiously to the story of St. Phillip's missionaries, remarking that if the Apostle was himself in Gaul, it is not impossible that he sent preachers to Britain. But if he cannot altogether accept the tradition of its foundation in the first century, he does testify to the great antiquity of the religious settlement on the Tor. He had himself seen a charter granted to it in A.D. 601 by a king of

Dumnonia, and he tells us that the wattle church was covered
with wooden boards by Paulinus, Bishop of Rochester, in the first
half of the seventh century. He believed also that St. Patrick was
one of the early Abbots of Glastonbury and died there in A.D. 472,
and that Gildas, the embittered historian of the Saxon conquest,
had sought sanctuary within the monastery from the troubles of
his time.

The destruction of this ancient Christian shrine, hallowed alike
by religion, history and legend, was an irreparable loss to the
devout, for which no new buildings, however magnificent, could
compensate. Nevertheless, the monks set to work to repair the
damage as far as that was possible. With the help of generous
gifts from Henry II they raised a new chapel of Our Lady on the
old site, and began to build another and much larger church a
little to the east of it. In 1189 the King died. His successor,
Richard I, needed all the money he could find for the Crusade
and had none to spare for abbeys at home, and the monks, already
deprived of their most illustrious shrine, were thus left to struggle
with diminished revenues and prestige, a burden of debt, and the
problem of raising funds for the completion of their unfinished
church.

Faced with these difficulties they may well have looked about
for some means of bettering the situation, and have sought to turn
the vague traditions of the district to good account. Even without
visions and ancient writings, there was some reason for supposing
that Arthur might be buried at Glastonbury, if he was buried at
all. Giraldus tells us that he had had a particular devotion to
Our Lady of Glastonbury and had made many gifts to the church.
If he had any say in the matter it is quite probable that he would
have chosen to lie near the Old Church, in the sacred spot where
British Christianity first began and where so many saints had
afterwards gathered. Moreover, tradition associated Glastonbury
with Avalon. The latter was almost certainly a supernatural
region in the original legends; the earliest writers never tell us
where it was, because it was not in this world. But Glastonbury,
that high and lonely island in a waste of marshes, could easily be
confounded with it. It was probably a sacred place long before
Christianity made it so, and as such connected in early thought

with the underworld. Giraldus says it was anciently called *insula Avallonia*, and he adds that it was "to the island which is now called Glastonbury" that Arthur was brought to be healed of his wounds. If this was the tradition in his day, the monks would certainly have known of it, and for those who did not believe in the undying hero legend it can only have meant that he was buried there.

On a certain day, therefore, the ground between the stone pyramids was enclosed with curtains, and the digging began. The hollowed oak which contained the bones was found at a great depth, resting upon a stone to which was fixed a leaden cross, with an inscription turned inwards: *Hic jacet sepultus inclitus rex Arthurus cum Wenneveria uxore sua secunda in insula Avallonia.* So, at least, says Giraldus,[1] who saw it, though other eye-witnesses give other wordings. Giraldus is the only writer who mentions that Guinevere was Arthur's second wife. Her bones lay at the foot of the great coffin, with a lock of golden hair, still fresh and bright, which crumbled to dust when it was touched. On Arthur's skull were the marks of ten wounds, all healed except one, from which presumably he died. His bones were enormous, the shin-bone coming well above the knee of the tallest man present. The remains were taken from the grave and laid in two coffers, in a black marble tomb with lions at each end and Arthur's image at the foot. Here in 1278 Edward I and Queen Eleanor saw them, when they came to spend Easter at Glastonbury, and ordered the opening of the tomb, which then stood in a chapel near the south door of the greater church, and was later removed to a spot in front of the high altar.

The leaden cross was carefully preserved, and Leland saw it when he visited the Abbey in Henry VIII's reign. He records the inscription as *Hic jacet sepultus inclitus rex Arturius in insula Avallonia;* another eye-witness, quoted by Ussher, says it was *Hic jacet gloriosissimus rex Britonum Arthurus.* It seems curious that no two accounts of the inscription agree, except in describing Arthur as a king, which in all probability he was not. Leland also records that Pomparles Bridge, between Glastonbury and Street, was in his day "caullid *Pontperlus*, wher men fable that *Arture* cast in his

---

[1] *De Principis Instructione* (c. 1194).

Swerd." This tradition, which would place the Battle of Camlan in Somerset, was still known in the district in 1924 when Mrs. Wood wrote her *Somerset Memories and Traditions*.

Arthur's tomb has disappeared now, like the print of his seal "in red wax closed in beryl" which Leland says was kept in Westminster Abbey, and the leaden cross which was last heard of in the eighteenth century in the possession of the Hughes family, of Wells. His sword, perhaps found in the Glastonbury grave, is said to have been given by Richard II to Tancred of Sicily; a crown alleged to be his was ceded by the Welsh to Edward I in 1282. All these things have vanished, like Guinevere's golden hair. We still do not know for certain where the historical Arthur was buried, or whether the bones exhumed behind curtains were his or those of some other man. All that remains to us is an undying legend, quite unaffected by the discovery of the grave, the supposed Round Table at Winchester, and the countless rocks and caves, castles, hills and cairns which bear his name.

CHAPTER IV

KING ARTHUR IN FOLK-LORE

WHATEVER evidence of mortality the Glastonbury grave provided, it was not enough to shake the popular belief in Arthur's return. For the simple folk of England, and still more of Wales and Brittany, he remained the king who was and who was yet to be. Twenty-five years after the opening of the grave, Giraldus Cambrensis could write in *Speculum Justitiae*:

> The King will return in strength and power, to rule over the Britons, as they think, according to his wont; wherefore they await his coming even as the Jews their Messiah. . . .

In 1540 Leland found the people of South Cadbury, only a few miles from Glastonbury, still convinced that he dwelt with his host in the Hollow Hill of Cadbury Fort. The splendid tomb before the High Altar of the Abbey, which some of them must have seen, had not altered their belief, and the legend survived long after the tomb itself had disappeared. The very grave which should have destroyed the tradition for ever was made to bear witness to its truth by later writers, and in *Liber Rubeus Bathoniae* (A.D. 1428) we read:

> But for he skaped that batell y-wys,
> Bretons and Cornysch seyeth thus,
> That he levyth yut, parde,
> And schall come and be a kyng aye.

THE CELTIC LEADER

At Glastonbury on the queer
They made Artourez toumbe there,
And wrote with latyn vers thus,
Hic jacet Arthurus, rex quondam, rexque futurus.[1]

It is this version of the ever-varying inscription which Malory quotes in that nostalgic passage of his *Morte D'Arthur*, where he says:

> Some men say yet that King Arthur is not dead, but had by the will of our Lord Jesu into another place. And men say that he shall come again, and he shall win the holy cross. I will not say it shall not be so, but rather I will say here in this world he changed his life. But many men say there is written upon his tomb this verse, Hic jacet Arthurus Rex quondam Rexque futurus.

It seems as though the hope embodied in the legend was too strong to be defeated by the mere finding of some bones. For the Celtic communities of England, Arthur represented all that was glorious and wonderful in the past and all that might be hoped for in the future. He was the historical hero of the race and, at the same time, he was a link between the world of everyday and that other world of faerie and magic, so near and so real to the minds of our ancestors. He was the king who had lived and fought in this country and could still be met with, riding in our forests where, as Gervase of Tilbury tells us, the foresters sometimes saw him with his horsemen at midday or on nights of full moon. For the Welsh and Bretons he was all that and more; he was their inspiration and their hope in the long struggle against English and Angevin.

It is possible that Henry II hoped by the opening of the grave to destroy the belief in Arthur's return, with its political repercussions, but it is clear that he did not succeed. The evidence afforded by the bones and the inscription was largely ignored by all who did not wish to believe it, and in the course of years many came to think that only Guinevere had been found during that discreet exhumation behind curtains. What really caused the decline of the tradition was not proof that Arthur was dead like other men, but the passage of time and the gradual changes which finally united Briton, Norman and Saxon into one nation. When

[1] Early English Text Society, Vol. 2.

deliverance was no longer desired, men ceased to look for the deliverer. The story passed into the great body of national folk-lore and became something only half believed in rural districts, a tale lovely and magical and inspiring, but no longer a living force anywhere, capable of inflaming political passion or influencing the actions of men.

Arthur was said to rest in many different places. Even as far afield as Sicily a tale was told of a groom, sent to search on Mount Etna for a missing horse, who strayed through caves and gullies and came at last to a fair plain whereon was a great palace. Within it he saw Arthur lying upon a bed, and heard from him of his last battle with Modred and how his wounds broke afresh every year. Presumably he would not be free to return to this world until they were finally healed. Here clearly Arthur is in Fairyland. The beautiful plain, full of delights, inside a mountain is reminiscent of that other lovely land under a river which the Welsh priest, Elidurus, visited, or the country beyond a cave from which the Green Children of Norfolk came. Another Etna story strikes a more ominous note. Arthur has become a king in the land of the dead. A groom in the service of the Dean of Palermo was sent to look for a horse, and was met by an old man who told him the animal was inside the mountain with King Arthur, whom he served. He then charged the groom with a message to the Dean, to the effect that he must present himself at Arthur's court within fourteen days. The message was delivered; the Dean laughed at it as nonsense, but within fourteen days he was dead. There are other legends which describe Etna as Purgatory or as Fairyland, but Arthur is not mentioned in them. He does not belong to Sicilian folk-lore, and his name was probably introduced by the Normans and attached by the local people to some already existing tradition.

In England and Wales, Arthur has several resting-places. In the late nineteenth century Mr. A. Clarke went with a party of archaeologists to Cadbury Fort, in Somerset, and was asked by an old man there whether he and his companions had come to take the King away. We know from the Reverend J. A. Bennett, a distinguished archaeologist and Rector of South Cadbury for twenty-four years, that at least as late as 1890 Arthur was believed to be within the fort. It was generally thought that the hill was hollow and that iron gates led into it. A vague tradition said that whoever ventured to ascend the hill on St. John's Eve would see something strange, but what this was no one seemed to know. A local poem mentioned by Sir E. K. Chambers says that golden gates were then visible in the hill-side, and anyone looking through them would see the King and his courtiers sitting within. But this, at least as far as the material of the gates is concerned, seems to be a poetic embellishment of the local belief. The gates were usually described as being of iron and situated close to one of the original entrances to the Fort. By a curious freak of folk-memory the position of this entrance was correctly remembered, though Mr. Bennett says that both it and the road leading to it had been completely obliterated by ploughing and the planting of ash-trees some 250 years before his time.

The hill, like many other Arthurian localities, was associated with fairies, who formerly brought their corn up there from a field below. By 1890 they had gone, but the King remained. One of his parishioners told Mr. Bennett that:

> The fairies were obliged to leave when the bells were put into the church, and they left all their gold behind them; and it is a pity our squire won't dig into the hill, for there is a lot of gold in it; and folks do say that on the night of the full moon King Arthur and his men ride round the hill, and their horses are shod with silver, and a silver shoe has been found in the track where they do ride; and when they have ridden round the hill, they stop to water their horses at the Wishing Well.[1]

On Christmas Eve also, the King and his host rode down from the Fort to drink from a spring by Sutton Montis Church.

Leland mentions the finding of the silver horseshoe, which he says was picked up at some time within the memory of people then living at Cadbury. This seems to place the event in the reign of Henry VII, or the last years of Richard III. He believed the Fort to be the original Camelot; the villagers told him that Arthur had once lived there. The top of the Fort is still called King Arthur's Palace, and a well on the east side of the hill is known as King

---

[1] *Proceedings of the Somerset Archaeological and Natural History Society*, Vol. XXXVI.

Arthur's Well. An ancient trackway running towards Glastonbury is called King Arthur's Lane, or Causeway. Tradition says he went hunting along it, and a labourer who lived beside it told Mr. Bennett that he sometimes heard the King and his men riding down it on rough winter nights.

This nocturnal riding is interesting because it associates Arthur with the Wild Hunt which has left its traces on so many of our legends and ghost stories. In several other versions of the sleeping-hero story, Arthur has with him horses and hounds, but he does not use them; they wait with him until the hour of deliverance strikes. At Cadbury he seems to have inherited the mantle of the unhappy King Herla, the British king who, in the days before the Saxon invasion, went to the Pygmy King's wedding feast for what he thought was a few days, and found on his return that two hundred years had gone by, during which all his friends had died and his kingdom had been taken by the invader. Henceforth he and his followers rode through the West Country, desperately seeking their lost homes, and were sometimes seen by the inhabitants of the places through which they passed. Walter Map tells us that the whole band plunged into the River Wye and perished at the end of the eleventh century, though, according to another tradition, they still ride and must do so until Doomsday. Other heroes have been condemned to such nocturnal journeys, like Earl Gerald in Ireland, or the unknown Master of Hounds who troubles the Meon Hills on Christmas Eve and New Year's Eve. Arthur himself rode through the forests of Gloucestershire and elsewhere in the Middle Ages, as we have seen, but Cadbury seems to be the only place where the legend of his riding out persisted to so late a period as the nineteenth century.

The Somerset version is perhaps the simplest and most interesting of all that have survived. The embellishments found in other localities are missing; Arthur is in the Fort, but he is not sleeping or spellbound, and there is no horn or bell by which he can be awakened and summoned back to this world. No one is supposed to have had speech with him at any time, or to have passed through the iron gates to his resting-place. His appearances do not forebode evil, and his actions have as little effect upon living men as theirs upon him. Even the treasure which so often forms a part of sleeping-hero stories does not belong to him but to the fairies who once inhabited the district.

The place with which he is thus associated is one which he may well have known in real life. Cadbury Fort must formerly have been a place of great strategic importance, standing as it does near the borders of three counties, where the high lands fall away to the valley leading down to Glastonbury. It seems to have been used in Romano-British times, for Leland says that Roman coins were often turned up by the plough, and he was himself given some of the coins so found. Camden thought it was probably the scene of one of Arthur's battles, and it may well be that he availed himself of this stronghold, with its quadruple line of fortifications and its five or six ancient roads radiating from it. It is even possible that he did live there at some period during the twenty years of calm after Mount Badon. The remote ancestors of the villagers may actually have seen him riding down the hill-side, in peace or in war, as their descendants believed that he still did.

In their *Roman Britain and the English Settlements* R. G. Collingwood and J. N. L. Myres suggest that the secret of Arthur's success was the revival of the cavalry arm on the Roman pattern, mail-clad horsemen against whom the Saxon foot-soldiers were unable to prevail. The Celtic tribes of that period did not use cavalry, but a strong leader, who remembered the tradition of late Roman horsemen in their shirts of mail with arm- and leg-pieces attached, may have persuaded them to do so, and himself have raised and trained such a force. In later poetic writings such warriors became the mediaeval knights of chivalry, members of the brotherhood of the Round Table, who set forth from the King's court on countless noble quests and adventures. The real Arthur's followers must have been very different, but if he did, in fact, rely chiefly upon the use of armoured riders, as Collingwood and Myres suggest, at a period when such fighters were not usual in this country, it would perhaps account for the frequent mention of horses and horsemen as part of his entourage in the various places where he is said to sleep.

Farther north, in Cheshire, we find the iron gates and the horses once again. On Alderley Edge, a sharply rising wooded hill now partly built over but formerly quite unspoilt, there is an inn called the Wizard Inn. On this hill there are ancient Roman mine-workings in which knockings and curious sounds have sometimes been heard; on one side of it there is a Wishing or Holy Well into which bent pins are still occasionally dropped, according to the old ritual, and near which a holly tree once stood, on whose branches votive rags were hung.

The Arthurian story of Alderley Edge concerns a farmer from Mobberley who, on some undated occasion, took a white horse across it to sell in Macclesfield market. An old man stopped him on the Edge and offered to buy the horse; the farmer refused to let him have it, and was told he would not sell it that day. Nor did he. In the evening he returned by the same road and again met the stranger, who now put on a more authoritative air and ordered the surprised man to follow him. The farmer did so, and together they went through the trees and came at last to a rock on which the old man struck with a rod. Iron gates opened in the rock face, and the two passed within. A number of men lay sleeping there, and with them many white horses, one horse for each man. One, however, was missing, and it was to supply its place that the farmer's horse was needed. His guide told him that the sleeping men were King Arthur and his warriors who would not waken until George, son of George, was king. Then they would arise and return to save their country, though from what or from whom was not explained. The farmer's courage failed him completely at this news, and he fled, leaving his horse behind. He never saw it again, and since that day no one has ever been able to find the iron gates. The old man, raised to the rank of wizard and perhaps vaguely connected with Merlin in popular thought, is commemorated in the name of the Wizard Inn.

On the other side of England, in Yorkshire, an almost forgotten tradition connects Arthur with Freeborough Hill, near Castleton. This hill is shaped like a tumulus, though it is not one, and it is possibly for this reason that Arthur was thought to sleep within it. In Murray's *Handbook for Travellers in Yorkshire*, 1874, we are told that "the name indicates that the court of the Anglian 'Free-burgh' or Tything . . . used to assemble here." If this is so, the association between kings and law-giving may have helped to strengthen an older legend of Arthur, or have suggested the hill to later generations as a suitable resting-place for so great a leader.

But it is to Richmond Castle that we must look for the most famous Yorkshire legend of Arthur. Not far away, on the other side of the River Swale, is a large cave known as Arthur's Oven, and underneath the Castle Keep the King himself lies sleeping. A man named Potter Thompson is said to have encountered a stranger near the castle and to have been taken by him to an underground vault of enormous size in which a multitide of people lay sleeping on the ground. The stranger showed Thompson a sheathed sword and a horn and invited him to draw the one and blow the other. Had he done so, the sleepers would have been freed from the enchantment that bound them, but Thompson was not fated to be their deliverer. When the sword was half out of its sheath they all stirred and seemed about to rise. In a sudden terror he let the blade fall back, and the sleepers sank down once more to the ground. A voice cried sadly:

> Potter Thompson, Potter Thompson,
> If thou hadst either drawn
> The sword or blown the horn,
> Thou'd been the luckiest man
> That ever yet was born.

Tradition has it that no other opportunity of breaking the spell will occur before a definite, though unstated, time has gone by.

This is one of several versions in which some human action, nearly always the drawing of a sword, or the sounding of a horn or bell, is necessary to free the enchanted king and his host. Potter Thompson was obviously taken to the vault for the express purpose of breaking the spell, though why he should have been chosen is not at all clear. In most cases the visitor finds the resting-place by accident and is either told by its occupants what to do, or meddles with the sword or horn from curiosity, until terror stops him. There is a Scottish story in which the sleeper is sometimes said to be King Arthur and sometimes Thomas the Rhymer, though the many points of similarity with other Arthurian legends suggest that Arthur was the original hero of the tale. A horse dealer sold a black horse to an aged man and was told to bring the animal at midnight to a hillock called the Lucken Hare, in the Eildon Hills.

He did so, and, more fortunate than the Cheshire farmer, he was paid the sum agreed upon, though in ancient coin. He then followed the old man into a cavern full of stalls, in each of which was a horse with a man in armour asleep at its feet. His guide told him that all would awaken at the Battle of Sheriffmuir, unless some person could be found bold enough to blow a horn and draw a sword that hung at the end of the cave. The dealer took down the horn and tried to wind it; immediately all the horses stamped in their stalls and shook their bridles, and the armoured men sprang up. Startled by the noise, he dropped the horn, and was blown out of the cave by a whirlwind, while a reproachful voice accused him of cowardice because he had not drawn the sword before he blew the horn.

At Sewingshields Castle, near the Roman Wall, there are two legends. A farmer knitting on the castle ruins dropped his clew and saw it fall into a subterranean passage. He followed it till he came to a large vaulted hall, with carved walls and a fretted roof. In the centre was a great fire burning without fuel, before which lay thirty couple of hounds. All round the room were thrones and couches, and on them slept Arthur and Guinevere and all their courtiers. A stone sword lay on a table with a garter and a horn beside it. The farmer drew the sword, and as he did so, the King and his companions awoke. He then cut the garter but, whether from fright or ignorance, replaced the sword before he had blown the horn. At once the spell descended again upon all the company and they fell asleep, the King saying before he closed his eyes:

> O woe betide that evil day
> On which this witless wight was born,
> Who drew the sword—the garter cut,
> But never blew the bugle-horn.

In the other Sewingshields story a shepherd went to search for a strayed sheep and found a ball of thread amongst the moss-covered stones of the castle. He followed it into a cavern which opened into a vestibule with a large room beyond. In this room an immense fire was blazing, with a huge cauldron upon it. Two hounds lay sleeping on either side of the hearth, and near it a table covered with a green cloth bore the usual horn and sheathed sword. The only human occupant of the room was an old man in armour, lying asleep in a chair. The shepherd lifted the horn, the hounds awoke, the old man sat up. He promised the shepherd that if he would blow the horn and draw the sword he would make him a knight to last through time. But the man had not the courage to do it alone; he went away to find a companion, and when he returned he could find no trace of the cavern that led into the inner hall.

The thread or clew and the immense fire are interesting points in these two stories, for both are well-known ingredients of folk-tales. It is probable that the cauldron mentioned in the shepherd's tale originally occurred also in the other, but was forgotten later in the telling. The hounds also seem to be an integral part of the Northumberland tradition. The second and infinitely sadder story of the lonely king, asleep in his great hall, with only four faithful hounds to bear him company, may perhaps be all that was remem-bered of the earlier splendid tale of the great host awaiting deliverance together round their magical fire, the thirty couple of hounds sharing their enchantment as they had once shared their pleasures. In the late nineteenth century the castle vaults were examined and removed by their owner, but nothing of any interest was found in them.

In many Arthurian resting-places hoards of treasure were thought to be hidden. Such hoards may once have been supposed to belong to the hero, who probably inherited them from the earlier spirit-inhabitants of the hill or cave, but in some of the later legends the ownership is not made clear. At Cadbury, as we have seen, the gold was left by the fairies. At Richmond Castle there was a Gold Tower or Gold Hole, so named because treasure was said to have been found there once, but who put it there in the first place is not recorded. At Sewingshields the owner's wife dreamt that she saw a hoard under the castle, and was so impressed by the vividness of her dream that she engaged workmen to dig amongst the ruins. Nothing was found, though the work went on for several days before hope was abandoned.

At Craig-y-Dinas, in Glamorganshire, a curious legend makes Arthur and his warriors the guardians of two heaps of precious metals. A Welshman was once walking over London Bridge with a hazel staff in his hand. He met a stranger, a cunning-man, who told him there was treasure under the tree from which his staff had been cut. The two men returned together to Wales, and found under the tree a cavern in which slept Arthur, wearing his crown, and all his men. In a passage leading to the cave hung a bell; if anyone struck it the heroes would awaken and return to this world, to lead the Welsh to victory. The cunning-man warned his companion that he must on no account touch the bell, but that if he did so, and the sleepers asked "Is it day?" he must at once reply "Nay, sleep thou on."

The warriors slept in a wide circle, in the centre of which were two heaps, one of gold and the other of silver. The Welshman was told he might take as much as he would, but only from one heap. This he did, and on leaving he accidentally touched the bell. The sleepers awoke and cried "Is it day?" but when the proper reply was given, they fell asleep again, and the Welshman retreated in safety with his pockets full of gold. Some time later, however, he returned for more. Again he struck the bell, and again the warriors asked their question. But this time he forgot the answer, and they all closed in upon him, took away his gold, and beat him so severely that he was a cripple for the rest of his life. The entrance to the cave was never found again.

Arthur sleeps in several other places in Wales. He is at Ogo'r Dinas and at Pumsaint and also at Caerleon, where the amphitheatre was long known as his Round Table. In the Snowdon district his men sleep in a cave, but he is not with them. He lies under a cairn in Bwlch y Saethau where, according to local tradition, he fell whilst driving his enemies up the pass from Cwmllan. A cave in Anglesea is said to have been his refuge during a war with the Goidels; probably it was once regarded as one of his mystical abiding places also. In Cornwall he lives in the form of a raven or, according to some versions, a Cornish chough. It was formerly considered very unlucky, if not actually wrong, to kill these birds, and a visitor to Marazion in the eighteenth century was sharply rebuked by the inhabitants for doing so. In Scotland, as we have seen, he sleeps in the Eildon Hills.

Many Arthurian place-names show clearly that the hero has become the heir of the giants in folk-belief. Legend has it that he fought with them, and he seems to have shared some of their more marvellous attributes. A Cornish tradition says that the county was full of these malicious beings until King Arthur drove them away. Near Camelford there is a barrow which is sometimes called Arthur's Grave and sometimes the Giant's Grave. The latter is probably the older name. At Camelford also is Slaughter Bridge, where an inscribed stone, nearly ten feet long, is known as Arthur's Tomb. It has been moved from its original place and the weatherworn letters upon it deciphered. They record that Latinus, the son of Magarius, lay beneath the stone. He may have been one of Arthur's followers, or a Romano-British warrior who fought in some other war. But for the local people the stone was clearly Arthur's, its length bearing out the tradition of his great height, and its situation the legend that Camelford was the site of the Battle of Camlan.

Curiously shaped rocks and odd markings upon stones were frequently ascribed to giants, and here too Arthur has inherited some of their traditions. Hollows worn by weather on the face of Tintagel Head are his Cups and Saucers; his Bed on Bodmin Moor is formed by a number of rocky tors. His Quoit in Cornwall is the capstone of a cromlech, and another cromlech near Dorston, in Herefordshire, is known as Arthur's Stone. Near Sewingshields, the King's Crag and the Queen's Crag are the highest points on two sandstone ridges about a quarter of a mile apart. Here Arthur and Guinevere sat talking, one on each crag, while the Queen combed her hair. Angered at something she had said, the hero threw a rock at his wife, an action more suited to the uncouth race of giants than to the chivalrous king. She caught it on her comb, and it fell between the ridges. Dr. Bruce tells us that it is still there "with the marks of the comb upon it, to attest the truth of the story. It probably weighs about 20 tons."[1] Not far off there was formerly a basaltic column, about ten feet high, with a natural seat on its top, which was locally known as King Arthur's Chair, or sometimes as King Ethel's Chair.

At Rhuthyn, in Denbighshire, is a stone called Maen Huail on which Huail, son of Kaw, was supposed to have been executed by Arthur's order. According to a Welsh tradition Arthur and Huail

[1] Dr. Bruce, *Wallet-Book of the Roman Wall.*

both fell in love with the same lady and fought over her. Arthur was wounded in the thigh and thereafter always limped slightly. He forgave Huail on condition that he swore never to refer to the matter again, or taunt his victim with the injury he had inflicted. Some time later Huail saw Arthur dancing and made a mocking remark about his lameness; for this breach of his oath he was beheaded on the stone which then lay in Rhuthyn street.

On Cefyn Carn Cavall, in the Builth district, there is a cairn bearing a stone with a mark upon it which was formerly supposed to be the footprint of Arthur's dog. The word *cafall* means a horse, and it is probable that the mark was originally thought to be the hoofprint of his famous mare, Llanrei, like the mark on Arthur's Stone at Flint. In his account of the wonders of Britain, Nennius tells us that:

> There is another marvel in the district which is called Buelt. Here is a pile of stones and on the top of the heap is a single stone with the footprint of a dog in it. When they hunted the pig Troynt, Cabal, who was the dog of the warrior Arthur, set his footprint in the stone, and Arthur afterwards made a heap of stones beneath the stone in which his dog's footprint was, and it is called Carn Cabal. And men come and bear off the stone in their hands during the space of a day and a night, and on the morrow it is found upon its heap.

In the middle of last century, Lady Guest persuaded a friend to visit Cefyn Carn Cavall and see if the stone was still there. He reported that there were several cairns on the mountain, and that on one lay a stone with an oval indentation on one side which "might without any great strain of imagination be thought to resemble the print of a dog's foot." He thought it probable that this was the actual stone referred to by Nennius, and added that as it was a species of conglomerate the mark might be "nothing more than the cavity left by the removal of a rounded pebble which was once imbedded in the stone."[1]

Arthur's dogs are commemorated again at Callington, where some rocky basins are called his Troughs, from which his dogs fed. Near by is Arthur's Hall. At St. Columb a stone bears four hoofprints of his horse. Near Zennor is a flat stone at which the hero

---

[1] Note to *The Mabinogion*, Lady Guest's translation.

sat to dine with four Cornish kings before the Battle of Vellan Drucher. In this case the enemy is said to have been, not the Saxons, but the Danes, who had landed in Whitesand Bay. At Longford Bridge, in Manchester, the pedestal of an ancient cross was long pointed out as a stone thrown by one of Arthur's foes, the champion, Sir Tarquin, who threw it from Knott Mill, two miles away. This man, who is usually described as a giant, lived in a castle made from the ruins of Roman Manchester and, after capturing many of Arthur's followers, was defeated by Sir Lancelot.

Guinevere has not fared so well in folk-tradition as her husband. In the Welsh Triads she is celebrated as one of the three lovely ladies of Arthur's court, and in *The Lady of the Fountain* the highest compliment that Kynon can pay to the maidens who wait upon him is to say they are more beautiful than Guinevere. But it is the legend of her frailty that has made the deepest impression upon folk-belief, though the legend itself springs from the later chivalric romances, and not from earlier writings, or the ancient traditions of the people. In parts of Wales it is, or was, an insult to call a girl a Gwenhwyvar, and a couplet still current there during the last century refers to her as:

> Gwenhwyvar, the daughter of Gogyrvan the Giant,
> Bad when little, worse when great.

In Cornwall the sound of waves beating on Boskenna rocks is said to be Jennifer weeping, and at Sewingshields we have already seen her, if not as an unfaithful, at least as a disrespectful wife, whose racial characteristics are of those the evil tribe of giants rather than of the noble Roman or Celtic family from which she is elsewhere said to have sprung.

The Welsh and Cornish traditions of Modred's raid upon Gelliwig and his abduction of the queen make her an unwilling victim, but there is a Scottish story which at least infers that she was a consenting party. Bury Hill, in Strathmore, is supposed to be the castle to which Modred brought her, and from which Arthur rescued her after the defeat of his nephew. As a punishment for her infidelity he ordered her to be torn in pieces by wild horses and her dismembered body to be buried in four different places.

In Meigle churchyard is Ganore's Grave, where a carving depicting a human form bound to the wheels of a chariot is said to mark one of these places. Arthur appears in this story as an inhuman savage and his wife as a wanton, and it may be noted that in many Scottish legends sympathy tends to be with Modred and his Pictish father, Lot, rather than with Arthur. In Boece's *Scotorum Historia* (1527), the British leader is both a usurper of the throne of Britain and devoid of all knightly virtues. He grossly deceives his nephew, and it is his treachery, rather than Modred's, which is the first cause of the war in which both fall. After her husband's death Guinevere is taken to Scotland as a prisoner and there she dies after long years of captivity.

All this is a far cry from the Glastonbury tomb and the bright lock of hair which preserved the memory of her beauty for more than six hundred years. The twelfth-century monks were willing to believe that she died peacefully, after many years of widowhood spent in a convent, and was united once more to her husband in the grave. And quite possibly they were right, whether that grave was at Glastonbury or elsewhere. The mediaeval romancers have been hard on Arthur's wife and have left her with a reputation for wantonness which she may not have deserved. There is, at least, no reliable evidence that it was deserved, and it may be that the Age of Chivalry, with its loose romantic notions and its preoccupation with *amour courtois*, has done less than justice to her memory.

CHAPTER V

ROBIN HOOD

ROBIN HOOD was essentially a people's hero. He was an outlaw, constantly at odds with authority; he was a successful robber and the avowed enemy of the rich and powerful. He defied the tyrannous Forest Laws of his day and openly filled his woodland larder with the King's game, which it was death for lesser men to touch. Though he had lost his own lands and his position in society he yet lived in freedom and comfort and, if the *Lytell Geste* is to be trusted, so loved his wild life that after being pardoned and restored to favour he fled from the King's court and of his own accord returned to the greenwood. Tradition declares that he was a true friend to the poor, who shared in the material profits of his robberies and were constantly heartened by his daring and impudent exploits against the rich. To the villein and the serf he must have seemed the very embodiment of that spirit of revolt against things as they are, that desire to level inequalities and to live an untrammelled life which springs eternally in the hearts of those to whom the world has been ungenerous, and never more vigorously than in the Middle Ages, when so many were bound by harsh laws and oppressed by a poverty from which it was extremely difficult to escape.

That he was not himself of humble birth did not matter. His lineage is more than uncertain, like many other details of his story. He is described in some early ballads as a yeoman, in others as a dispossessed Earl. In either case he was not a poor man, but his defiance of accepted authority and his cheerful disregard of property rights were enough to make him the hero of every rebel or would-be rebel of his own and later times. Farther on in history the same inarticulate discontents were to enshrine such doubtful characters as Dick Turpin and other highwaymen in national legend, but whatever the true Robin Hood may have been, he was less sordid than these. There is a vigour and gaiety about his traditions which is lacking in those of the later thieves, and there is no evidence that he was ever gratuitously cruel, as they sometimes were, or at least, any more so than most men were in his day.

Of all the English hero-legends, his is perhaps the most doubtful and confused. Many writers have asserted that no such person ever existed and that he represents only the remains of ancient pagan or fairy beliefs. Thomas Wright in *Essays on the Literature of the Middle Ages* calls him "one amongst the personages of the early mythology of the Teutonic peoples". W. H. Stevenson says his whole story is "a mediaeval myth, sprung from the mists of Teutonic Paganism, garnished by the prolific muses of the English minstrels . . ."[1], and Sir Sidney Lee in the *Dictionary of National Biography* describes him as a forest elf who was so named because elves wore hoods. Margaret Murray[2] suggests that Robin Hood was the title to Grandmasters of the witch-cult, the name in this case meaning "Robin with a Hood", in reference to an important part of the ceremonial attire worn by such officials at the Sabbats. The Grandmasters represented the god of the cult and bore his name, as did the lesser chiefs of covens in their absence. This god was known by many names, and one of them seems to have been Robin. The Somerset witches in 1664 called "Robin" when they wished to summon the Chief of their coven, and in 1324 Dame Alice Kyteler admitted that she worshipped a spirit named Robin Artisson. The fairy known as Robin Goodfellow was closely associated with the Devil, and probably started life,

---

[1] W. H. Stevenson, *Notes about Nottinghamshire.*
[2] M. Murray, *The God of the Witches.*

not as a fairy, but as one of the many forms taken by the Horned God of witchcraft. A tract published in 1638 shows him as a horned figure dancing on goat's feet in the centre of a ring of witches. As Robin Goodfellow he is mentioned in an old charm against evil spirits, but Keightley tells us in his *Fairy Mythology* that he had other names. One of these was Robin Hood.

Other writers accept the possibility that the legends were founded upon memories of actual human beings, but believe that there were several "Robin Hoods", and that forest robbers and outlaws frequently called themselves by that name. It has been suggested that Robin was a generic title for such men, and that Hood is not a true surname, but a corruption of "O' th' wood". Dr. Stukeley, who regards the famous bandit as an historical personage, maintains that his real name was Robert Fitzooth, and that Robin Hood was merely the name by which he was commonly known. If, in fact, there was such an individual in the Middle Ages he may have been only the best known amongst many who bore a nickname perhaps originally associated with the Horned God, or with fairies and later transferred to those who also haunted the forests, though for other reasons and in a different manner.

A Statute of Edward III's reign refers to "divers manslaughters, felonies and robberies done in times past by people that be called Roberdsmen, wasters and drawlatches," but whether "Roberds-men" is a direct reference to Robin Hood's band, or a general term for criminals of this class is not clear. That the Nottingham-shire hero early became the traditional type of woodland outlaw is shown by a reference to him which appears in the Rolls of Parliament in 1437. In that year a petition was presented for the arrest of Piers Venables, of Derbyshire, on the grounds that he had effected a rescue by violence and had then taken to robbery, going "into the woods in that country, like as it had been Robyn Hood and his meynie." The outlaw who figured in so many popular ballads would doubtless have many imitators, and later robbers may well have adopted a name so famous in their calling, or have had it bestowed upon them by their admirers, whether it originally belonged by right to a single individual or a spirit, or was nothing more than a traditional title for a particular type of woodland thief.

73

Moreover, those who took part in Robin Hood plays were often known by the names of the characters they habitually portrayed, and this fact almost certainly led to later confusion between actors and originals. Fabyan mentions in his *Chronicle* the arrest of a felon "wyche had renued many of Robyn Hodes pagentes", and called himself Grenelefe, as Little John once did to deceive the Sheriff of Nottingham. A certain Robert Stafford, of Lindfield, Sussex, seems to have been known as Friar Tuck in the early fifteenth century, for he is so described in the *Calendar of Patent Rolls*, 1429–36, where his pardon for failing to answer a summons for trespass is recorded. Joseph Hunter[1] believes that the supposed grave of Little John at Hathersage did not contain the bones of that hero, but merely those of some local man who had won fame as an actor in the plays. He quotes a note on the subject written by Dodsworth in the seventeenth century which refers to a certain Robert Lockesley, of Bradfield in Hallamshire, who

> . . . wounded his stepfather to death at plough, fled into the woods, and was relieved by his mother till he was discovered. Then he came to Clifton-upon-Calder, and came acquainted with Little John that kept the kine; which said Little John is buried at Hathersage in Derbyshire, where he hath a fair tombstone with an inscription. Mr. Long saith that Fabyan saith Little John was an Earl Huntingdon. After, he joined with Much, the Miller's son.

"Little John that kept the kine" does not sound like an outlaw, though if he was styled "an Earl Huntingdon" he may have been one, or have been connected with hunting and forest life in some other way. Robin Hood was traditionally supposed to be the rightful Earl of Huntingdon, and his followers may have been so nicknamed. Gutch, however, says that the phrase was used at one time to describe any skilled huntsman. Dodsworth's note does not make it clear whether Robert Lockesley's acquaintance was the original Little John or merely someone who was so called, either because of his acting or for some other reason. If he was, in fact, an actor in the plays, it is possible that he was chosen for that particular part on account of his great height. The Hathersage grave is 13 ft. 4 in. in length, and Ritson[2] tells us that when it

[1] Reverend J. Hunter, *Critical and Historical Tracts, No. IV.*
[2] J. Ritson, *Robin Hood.*

was opened it was found to contain bones of an unusual size, amongst them a thigh-bone 29½ in. long. He also mentions a local tradition which says that after the removal of the remains, dire misfortune overtook both the man who ordered the exhumation and the sexton who did the actual work, and that these troubles ceased only after the bones had been reverently replaced.

Hathersage is very near the Yorkshire border, and it is quite possible that the original Little John and his companions were seen there during their lives; some of them may even have been Derbyshire men. Near the churchyard is a cottage in which Little John is supposed to have died peacefully after his long and turbulent life in the forest; not far from the village is a well called after Robin Hood, and two stone-lows on the Grindleford road are known as Robin Hood's Pricks. But it must be remembered that other places besides Hathersage claim to be Little John's resting-place, and while he may have had some connexion with the district and may perhaps have died there, it is equally possible that the tall man who lies in the churchyard is not the hero himself but some actor or imitator, once locally renowned but now completely forgotten and absorbed into the legends of his famous original.

The Robin Hood plays were closely connected with morris dancing and the ancient ceremonies of May Day, and this fact has strengthened the belief of those who hold that Robin Hood himself never existed in the flesh, but was a mere relic of paganism. It has been suggested also that the entire cycle of legends sprang directly from the May-games and from the characters in the plays acted at that season. This seems hardly probable, however, in view of the persistent belief in Robin Hood's actual life in this country, a belief which has endured for centuries and has flowered in a host of legends of very varying nature, as well as in a crop of place-names and proverbs. No doubt the performances kept his memory green as nothing else could have done, just as the constant stream of new ballads and the exploits of his imitators added continually to the long list of his heroic deeds. No doubt also the memory of those who played the different parts became in time confused with that of his followers, so that their houses or graves were sometimes pointed out as those of the robbers themselves. But this is not to say that the plays were responsible for the Robin Hood saga in the first place, or that every spot associated with the outlaw and his band commemorates nothing more than some forgotten actor. On this theory England should be full of traditional graves or dwellings, for the plays were acted in every part of the country. It is more probable that they were incorporated in the May ceremonies precisely because they were based on stories already well known and believed to be true, and because they presented incidents in the life of a popular hero, of whose former existence no member of the audience had any doubt whatever.

We cannot be so sure to-day that Robin Hood really lived, as were those far-off audiences, for we have nothing upon which to rely but a few surviving plays and ballads and the strong traditions of the countryside. Nothing in his recorded life is certain. His rank and lineage are alike disputed; his birthplace cannot be definitely fixed; even the period in which he lived has been a matter for controversy. History is silent concerning him, and the only sure thing about this enigmatic hero is his enduring hold upon the imagination of English people from at least as early as the fourteenth century down to the present day. Nevertheless, if tradition is our only guide, the very strength of that tradition may give us pause. When every negative theory has been examined, there still remains the possibility that behind the mists of contradiction and uncertainty moves the shadowy figure of an actual human being who once lived and robbed his fellow-men in the then wild forests of Sherwood and Barnesdale.

The Forest Laws of the Middle Ages were extremely severe and were proportionately hated. Any man who could successfully defy them would be certain of popularity with all but those whose duty or interest lay in enforcing them. Such a man would have many sympathizers amongst the country people, who would joyfully repeat every story of despoiled nobles, narrow escapes from justice, or daring rescues of fellow-criminals, that was told about him. The natural desire to chronicle the discomfiture of the rich and powerful would ensure that such tales were not quickly forgotten, nor would they lose anything in the telling. A brief study of the surviving ballads shows that single incidents are often repeated

Robin Hood: the Outlaw Hero

with varying detail, so that the outlaw seems to deceive or kill the sheriff, or rescue companions from the Nottingham gallows, not once but many times. It is, of course, highly improbable that any one man could have performed all the startling acts ascribed to Robin Hood, and that he should have lived so dangerous a life unscathed until the advanced age of eighty-seven is almost incredible. But when due allowance is made for exaggerations and embroideries, it is possible that some at least of the tales are founded upon fact. A single daring exploit would provide matter for a dozen laudatory stories and confirm the people's instinctive admiration for a courageous rebel. And if, by judicious kindnesses, the outlaw made allies of humble folk who could help him by passing on information or concealing stolen goods, it would not be long before he was regarded as the protector of the oppressed, a man whose robberies were not morally wrong, since he took from the rich to benefit the poor and aided serfs and villeins in their struggle for freedom. That the real Robin Hood, if he existed, was any less selfish than other professional thieves is not very likely, but if he had the wit to make friends of those who were not worth robbing, his crimes would be easily glossed over by his admirers and only his benefactions remembered.

He is usually supposed to have flourished in the reign of Richard I, but even this has been questioned. The *Sloane MS.* says he was born in 1160, and Thoresby in *Ducatus Leodensis* records his death at Kirklees Priory in 1247 when, if the first date is correct, he would have been eighty-seven years old. Gutch, on the other hand, gives his birth date as 1225. Hunter believes him to have been a Yorkshire man, born at Wakefield between 1285 and 1295, and one of those who took part in the Earl of Lancaster's rebellion against Edward II in 1322. The defeat of the rebels at Boroughbridge was followed by wholesale banishments and confiscation of estates, and it is possible that the Robert Hood who is mentioned in the Court Rolls of the Manor of Wakefield for 1316 may have lost his property then and, as Hunter suggests, have taken to the woods to escape the King's vengeance. The *Lytell Geste* describes his meeting with "Edward our comly kynge", but does not make it clear which King Edward is meant. In this ballad the King disguises himself as a monk, knocks down the outlaw with one blow, and then persuades him to leave the greenwood and come to court. Robin consents; his confiscated lands are restored to him, and he is treated with marked favour. But he pines for the wild life of the forest and, having obtained permission to revisit Barnesdale for one week only, he gathers his band round him once more and refuses to leave the forest again.

History gives some faint support to this story. The ballad states that the King came to Lancashire for the express purpose of capturing the outlaw, but was so impressed by his courtesy and courage that he pardoned him instead. At the end of 1323 Edward II went on a progress through Lancashire, and afterwards stayed for some weeks in Nottingham. In 1324 a man named Robin or Robert Hood seems to have been Groom of the Chamber for a few months, and Hunter thinks this may have been the famous outlaw. But whoever he was, he did not hold office for long. He remained at court only from March to November, and was then discharged as being no longer able to work. This is a less romantic explanation of his departure than that given by the ballad, but the presence at court of a man so named, at that particular period and for so short a time, does suggest at least a foundation for the unknown poet's story.

On the whole, however, the earlier dates seem the more probable. Fordun[1] mentions both Robin Hood and Little John in 1341, whence we may conclude that their names were already known in England at that time. In *The Vision of Piers Plowman*, written about 1360, a drunken priest confesses that he cannot repeat the Lord's Prayer, but he can "rhyme of Robin Hood and Randulph, Earl of Chester." This suggests that songs and ballads based on the robber's life were popular in the middle of the fourteenth century, and presumably had been so for some time before the poem was written. The priest clearly expects his hearers to know of whom he speaks, and no doubt they did. But it must be remembered that Robin Hood was not at first a national hero in the sense that Arthur and Hereward the Wake had been. He was the leader of no great cause; he headed no desperate rising against foreign invader or native tyrant, such as might have made his name known and respected throughout England. His early

---

[1] John Fordun, *Scotichronicon*.

renown must have been purely local, for his main activities were confined to two counties only, and many of his contemporaries in other parts of the country may well have lived and died without ever hearing of him. A fairly considerable time would have been necessary for his legend to spread over the whole country from its original home in the Midlands and the North, and the short period between the Battle of Boroughbridge and the publication of *Piers Plowman* hardly seems sufficient. The "rhymes" mentioned by the priest were probably ballads current in his own day, but based upon older traditions, and this in itself suggests a more remote period for Robin Hood's life. None of these fourteenth-century ballads has come down to us; the earliest now surviving is the *Lytell Geste*, printed by Wynkyn de Worde at the end of the fifteenth century.

In *Palaeographia Britannica* Dr. Stukeley adheres to the earlier dates and supports the outlaw's claim to the earldom of Huntingdon by tracing his pedigree back through Philip, Lord of Kyme, to Waltheof, Earl of Northumberland, and Judith, niece of William the Conqueror. Waltheof was also Earl of Huntingdon by right of marriage, whence Robin Hood's supposed title was derived. Dr. Percy,[1] however, points out that the earlier ballads invariably call him a yeoman. The *Lytell Geste* certainly does, and it is only in later writings that he is "instiled Earl of Huntingdon, Lord Robin Hood by name." Grafton,[2] writing in 1569, mentions an "ancient pamphlet" that he once saw which combined both theories by saying that he was originally of base stock, but was raised to an earl's dignity for his chivalrous behaviour. Dr. Stukeley's detailed pedigree is full of noble names, but he gives no authority for his statements, and Robin Hood's noble birth must remain a matter of considerable doubt. It seems more probable that he was a free man of lesser rank who lost whatever property he possessed either, as the *Sloane MS.* asserts, through debts contracted during an undisciplined youth, or, as other authorities have it, through rebellion against the King, and thereafter took to the forest and the mediaeval form of highway robbery. Dr. Stukeley infers that he inherited a lawless strain, and says he

---

[1] Dr. Percy, *Reliques of ancient English Poetry.*
[2] Richard Grafton, *Chronicle*, 1569.

adopted "this wild way of life, in imitation of his grandfather Geoffrey de Mandeville, who being a favourer of Maud Empress K. Stephen took him prisoner at S. Albans, and made him give up the tower of London, Walden, Plessis, etc., upon which he lived on plunder."[1]

In a ballad which Dr. Percy thinks no older than the reign of Charles I, we are told that Robin Hood was born "in Locksly town, in merry Nottinghamshire". Tradition usually assigns him to that county, but it is by no means certain that he was actually born there. Dr. Fuller includes him amongst the "Memorable Persons of Nottinghamshire", but does not state that he was of Nottinghamshire stock; he tells us only that the outlaw belonged to the county by adoption, if not by birth, and adds:

> His principal residence was in Shirewood forest in this county, though he had another haunt (he is no fox that hath but one hole) near the sea in the North-riding in Yorkshire where Robin Hoods bay still retaineth his name: not that he was any pirat, but a land-thief, who retreated to those unsuspected parts for his security.[2]

The *Sloane MS.* says he was "borne in Lockesley in Yorkshire, or after others, in Nottinghamshire", but there is no place of that name in either county, though there is a Loxley in Staffordshire, near Needwood Forest. A writer in the *Gentleman's Magazine* for 1820 suggests that he was the son of William Fitzooth who held land at Loxley under the lordship of Robert de Ferrers, and that his father may have lost his estates by siding with de Ferrers when the latter rebelled against Henry II in 1173. Tutbury is here given as the scene of his youthful frolics, and perhaps the place where he amassed those debts which led to his subsequent outlawry. The ballad already mentioned says he was married there to a lady named Clorinda, whose surname and lineage are not given. Hunter, as we have seen, claims him for Yorkshire and makes him a citizen of Wakefield. In his *Sheffield Glossary* Addy quotes from a MS. survey made by John Harrison in 1637, which mentions "Little Haggar's croft, wherein is the foundation of a house or cottage where Robin Hood was born; this piece is

---

[1] Dr. Stukeley, MS. note in his copy of *Robin Hood's Garland*.
[2] Dr. Fuller, *Worthies of England*.

compassed about with Loxley firth . . ." His birthplace is thus extremely uncertain, but it seems clear that he was of North Midland or Yorkshire stock and that he frequented as an outlaw those woods and wild places which were already known to him in youth.

He is usually supposed to have married Matilda, or Maud, daughter of Robert, Earl Fitzwalter, who is buried in Little Dunmow Church and is better known to us as Maid Marion. This name she is said to have taken when she joined her husband in the forest. Stowe tells us in his *Annales* that she was called Maud the Fair and was loved by King John, whose suit she refused. Her father upheld her in this refusal and was consequently banished, and she herself was poisoned by the King's order. "Whilst Maud the faire remayned at Dunmow," says the chronicler, "there came a messenger unto her from king John about his suit in love, but because she would not agree, the messenger poysoned a boyled or potched egge against she was hungrie, whereof she died." This addition to the long list of John's crimes may or may not be founded upon fact, but the story as Stowe tells it makes no reference to Robin Hood. In 1601, however, it was incorporated in a play called *The Death of Robert, Earle of Huntingdon, otherwise called Robin Hood of merrie Sherwood; with the lamentable tragedy of chaste Matilda, his faire maide Marion, poysoned at Dunmowe by king John.* In this, Matilda lives in the forest with the robber band and shares Robin's leadership. She is not married to him, but is called Maid Marion to show that she is leading "a spotless maiden life" until his outlawry is ended and he can make her his wife. After his death she retires to Little Dunmow Priory, and is there poisoned by the disappointed King in the manner already related.

Unfortunately, there is no real evidence that Robin Hood was married to Matilda Fitzwalter or, indeed, to anyone else. If he had a wife at all, her name has not survived. The Robert Hood mentioned in the Wakefield Court Rolls of the early fourteenth century had a wife named Matilda, but she was certainly not Fitzwalter's daughter, for that lady had died many years before. The traditional association of these two famous people may perhaps be explained by the fact that, owing to the manner of her death, Matilda was regarded as an English heroine who withstood the

Norman tyrant and could easily be joined in popular fancy to that other rebel against oppression, Robin Hood. It is noteworthy that the earlier ballads do not mention her at all, either by her own or her traditional name, and she first appears as the outlaw's companion in *The Ship of Fools*, published in 1500. On the other hand, Maid Marion was an important character in the May-games, and in some places the chosen May Queen seems to have borne this title. It is, of course, possible that the name was conferred upon the queen in honour of Robin Hood's traditional mate; it is equally possible, and perhaps more probable, that Maid Marion was originally quite distinct from the Robin Hood saga and was only later incorporated with it. A "love interest" was doubtless as much appreciated in the Middle Ages as it is to-day, and to join in one legend the principal character of the May-games, and of the Robin Hood plays which formed part of them, was an easy method of providing one.

Of his male companions, the earliest mentioned is Little John, who was his second-in-command. Fordun refers to him in 1341, and he is named in the *Lytell Geste*, together with Gilbert of the White Hand, Much the Miller's son, and Will Scathelocke, or Scadlock. The last of these is said to have joined the robber band after Robin had kidnapped the girl he desired from the very church door, where she was being married to someone else against her will, and had caused the couple to be married in the forest, presumably by Friar Tuck. Grafton tells us that after his outlawry Robin Hood, "for a lewde shift, as his last refuge, gathered together a companye of roysters and cutters", and this would, no doubt, be a fairly accurate description of many of his followers, men of like mind with himself, who hated authority in any form and infinitely preferred the hazards of banditry to the restrictions of a conventional life. The *Sloane MS.* says that he first tested recruits by fighting with them and then, if they proved themselves strong and courageous, persuading them to join him. That militant cleric, Friar Tuck, was enrolled in this way and so was George a Green, the pinner of Wakefield. In his hey-day his followers are said to have numbered as many as 150, of whom the majority were skilled archers. This is almost certainly an exaggerated estimate, but he may well have been the leader of a small and well-organized band of men, whose daring, good markmanship and superior knowledge of the wilder parts of the country would enable them, aided as they almost certainly were by a host of sympathizers, to elude capture and defy the authorities for a considerable number of years.

A strong and persistent tradition says that Robin Hood died at Kirklees Priory in Yorkshire, and was buried in the woods near that house. In his old age, overcome by illness and trouble, he sought refuge and treatment in this convent, the Prioress of which was a woman of some medical skill. She is sometimes said to have been his aunt, in which case his choice of this obscure nunnery is easily understood. Whilst being nursed back to health he was bled and, either through treachery or accident, was allowed to bleed to death. Popular tradition inclines to the theory of murder, but is uncertain whether it was the work of the Prioress herself or a monk brought in to attend the patient. The *Sloane MS.* recounts how:

> being dystempered with cold and age, he had great payne in his lymmes, his bloud being corrupted, therefore to be eased of his payne by letting bloud, he repayred to the priores of Kyrkesly, which some say was his aunt, a woman very skylful in physic and surgery, who perceiving him to be Robyn Hood, and waying howe fell an enimy he was to religious persons, toke revenge of him for her owne house and all others by letting him bleed to death. It is also sayd that one Sir Roger of Doncaster, bearing a grudge to Robyn for some injury, incyted the priores, with whome he was very familiar, in such a maner to dispatch him.

The writer goes on to say that after his death she caused him to be buried by the roadside, and a place near the Three Nuns Inn is pointed out as the site of this unhallowed grave. The Prioress is clearly shown in this account as a vindictive and treacherous woman whose malice extended even beyond the death of her victim. But other legends say the blood-letting was done by an unnamed monk, and this man may have murdered his patient on his own account without her connivance or knowledge. In any case she is entitled to the benefit of a strong doubt, for it is not even certain that he was murdered at all. A nephew of eighty-seven presupposes an aunt at least elderly, if not already old, even if, as sometimes happens, she is younger than he is. Whatever may have been Robin's record in the past, it is surely not too much to hope that, when both were so advanced in age, the fires of revenge and hatred would have burnt themselves out long before. So old a man could hardly have been very dangerous to anyone, and even the most bloodthirsty individual might well hesitate before burdening his soul with murder when the proposed victim is already so near the grave. It seems more probable that his death was due to simple inefficiency on the part of the surgeon, or perhaps to his own inability to withstand the copious blood-lettings of that period while he was still weakened by illness.

However that may be, he died as the result of the operation. He chose his own resting-place by the characteristic device of shooting two arrows through the window and giving instructions that he was to be buried where they fell. The first went into the River Calder and was carried away by the stream; the second lighted in the park which surrounded the convent, and there his reputed grave stands, some five hundred yards from the farm-house which is all that now remains of the priory. Not far off are the graves of a child and of Elizabeth Stainton, once Prioress of the house, who may or may not have been the lady in question. These are the only graves still surviving, though there must once have been many more, since the nuns who died in the priory would naturally be buried in their own cemetery within the grounds. Thoresby tells us that in his day the inscription on Robin Hood's tombstone was illegible, but from a paper found amongst the effects of Dr. Gale, formerly Dean of York, he learnt that it ran as follows:

> Hear underneath dis laitl stean
> Lais Robert, earl of Huntingtun;
> Near arciv ver as hie sa geud
> An pepl kauld im Robin Heud.
> Sick utlaws as hi an is men
> Vil England nivr si agen.
> Obiit 24 Kal. Dekembris 1247.

The genuineness of this epitaph has been questioned by most writers, and it has been suggested that it was written by someone who tried to imitate the style of thirteenth-century writings and succeeded well enough to deceive the Dean. The stone itself is clearly in the wrong place, for Gutch tells us in *Sepulchral Monuments* that it was lifted on one occasion by order of Sir Samuel Armitage, and not only were no bones found beneath it, but the ground had obviously never been disturbed before. This does not, however, necessarily mean that tradition is wrong in placing Robin Hood's grave at Kirklees. No other site has ever been suggested, and the very persistent legend of his death in the priory is not improbable in view of his own association with the West Riding and the secluded and presumably safe situation of the convent. If, as seems probable, the stone was a later addition, whoever set it there may have been unaware of the exact location of the grave, and have placed it on the spot where the arrow was traditionally supposed to have fallen. Robin Hood himself may lie quite near it or, if his wishes were disregarded, he may rest among the now lost graves in the nuns' cemetery. It is not likely that the problem will ever now be solved, and those who visit the present tomb at Kirklees Priory Farm must content themselves with the thought that the hero's bones may be somewhere not far off, even though they are not in the actual place marked by the ancient stone and the iron railings which now surround it.

Uncertain as are the details of his career, Robin Hood's general characteristics stand out clearly from the mass of contradictory legends which have gathered round his name. He seems to have been a cheerful bandit, a hearty, boisterous, roystering man, with a violent but short-lived temper and an easy nature that could not harbour malice for long. If the ballads can be trusted, he was the possessor of an impish sense of humour; many of them recount the tricks he played on the Sheriff of Nottingham and others, and the disguises he loved to assume. He was always ready to engage in a fight and to challenge any man whom he considered suitable for enrolment in his band. He was quick to resent an insult; in *Robin Hood and the Beggar* we read that the latter's defiance so infuriated him that he attempted to shoot him, though the other man was armed only with a stick, and was soundly beaten for his pains. He struck his friend and lieutenant, Little John, because the latter claimed to have won five shillings from him at play; he "raged like a wild boar" when Arthur Bland, the tanner, drew blood during a fight. But he never bore malice when he was fairly defeated and easily forgave an injury, unless it was inflicted by a monk or a priest.

Dr. Fuller says he was "rather a merry than a mischievous thief (complementing passengers out of their purses), never murdering any but deer and . . . feasting the vicinage with his venison."[1] All the ballads insist that he was courteous and pious and had a great devotion to Our Lady; one says that for her sake he never harmed any company that had a woman in it. In *Robin Hood and the Monk* we are told that he made a special journey to Nottingham because he had not been able to hear Mass for a fortnight, and was there betrayed by a monk who saw him praying in St. Mary's Church. In the ensuing fight he killed twelve men single-handed and was only captured after he had broken his sword over the Sheriff's head. From this predicament he was rescued by Little John. The *Lytell Geste* relates that he once met an impoverished knight in Barnesdale Forest, who told him that his lands were mortgaged to St. Mary's Abbey in York and that he had no other friend but Our Lady who had never failed him until now. Robin replied that he could have no better surety, and lent him £400 to pay off the mortgage. The knight promised to repay him on an agreed date, but, being delayed, did not appear when he was expected. Robin, therefore, captured a number of monks from the abbey as they were riding on a journey, and forced them to pay the money on the ground that their patron had guaranteed the loan. In addition, because they pretended to have no gold with them, he took from them a further £400. When the knight finally arrived he not only forgave him the debt, saying that Our Lady had already paid it, but presented him with the extra £400 which he had taken from the monks.

He seems to have been a good and intelligent leader; his followers were devoted to him, and he, on his side, never failed them when they were in difficulties. His chief enemies were the clergy; for them he had an undying hatred, and it is for this reason that the Prioress of Kirklees is supposed to have murdered him. In the *Lytell Geste*, when Little John asks for instructions, Robin tells him that no member of the band must harm a husbandman

[1] Dr. Fuller, *Worthies of England*.

"that tylleth with his plough", or any yeoman, squire or knight, but that

> "These bysshoppes and thyse archebysshoppes
> Ye shall them bete and bynde"

and the same actute dislike was visited upon abbots and priors and the lesser clerics. Sheriffs and forest rangers were his natural foes, but it was for the clergy that he seems to have reserved a particular hatred which caused him to humiliate as well as rob them whenever he could. It is not clear whether he had any special reasons for this, or whether it was simply the distaste of the man of action for the scholar and the natural rebel's aversion to anything which represented law and authority. Miss Murray sees in it evidence of Robin Hood's association with the witch-cult, for the Grandmasters and coven chiefs who were the priests of that cult would naturally be at enmity with the Christian hierarchy. But Robin, for all his cleverness, seems to have been a simple soul, and probably his actions, as well as his likes and dislikes, were governed by simple feelings. Whatever he actually was, he has passed into our folk-lore as a roaring, jovial, hot-tempered and kind-hearted thief, to whom fighting and trickery were joys and freedom a necessity, the eternal type of the light-hearted rebel who cannot brook restriction, whether it be that of constituted authority or the more exacting demands of some revolutionary cause.

ROBIN HOOD PLAYS AND PLACES

ROBIN HOOD'S name is still a household word, seven
hundred years after his death. In spite of the uncertainty
which surrounds every detail of his career, he and his
followers are more familiar to us to-day than many an undoubtedly
historical individual for whose life-story reliable documentary evidence can be produced. We are reminded of him daily by a host of
Wells, Pricks, Butts, Chairs and Strides called after him, some of
which are to be found in places not otherwise associated with him
and where, in all probability, he never set foot. He has given his
name to such diverse things as a hedgerow flower, a bay on the
north-east coast, a thaw wind, and numerous Courts of the Ancient
Order of Foresters. When in 1929 a title was needed for the big
clock in the new Council House in Nottingham, it was unanimously decided to call it Little John, and the same jovial giant or
his master can still be seen on country inn-signs. This mediaeval
bandit, who never fought in any cause but his own or sacrificed
himself for any man, this jolly thief whose life of complete selfish-
ness was redeemed only by his cheery temperament and careless
generosity, is better remembered by most people than the heroic
Arthur or Hereward the Wake, or even St. George, with whom he

shared the honour of the principal part in the Mumming Plays. Every district with which tradition connects him in any way is proud to remember him, and his spirit is still vigorously alive in what remains of Sherwood Forest and the neighbourhood of Whitby.

The roots of his popularity lay in the fact that he was the embodiment both of the latent discontents of the Middle Ages and their ideal remedy. For this purpose it made little difference whether he was really, as seems probable, an historical character of the twelfth and early thirteenth centuries, or whether his name covers a number of otherwise anonymous rebels. The magic words "Robin Hood" conjured up a vision of successful revolt and freedom, no matter to whom or to what they were originally applied. But if he had been no more than the symbol of past grievances, it is unlikely that his fame would have become so widespread or endured for so long. He had the unique good fortune to be early associated with the May Day rites, those ancient ceremonies which were once enacted all over England, and in which he seems gradually to have superseded that now forgotten but formerly important character, the May King. Once popular tradition had transformed Maid Marion into his wife, it was an easy matter to confuse Robin Hood himself with the King of May who, no less than his partner, represented the summer and all its joys. The ceremonies began with the gathering of green boughs from woods and wild places, such as those in which the outlaw had once reigned supreme, and his own pleasure-loving character, as portrayed by the legends, made him eminently suitable for the chief part in rites which welcomed the season of plenty and freedom from winter's cares.

The Robin Hood games were given side by side with the May-games or at the Whitsun Ales. In the Churchwardens' Accounts of Croscombe, in Somerset, for the year 1506 the May feast is referred to as "the sporte of Robart Hode". In this parish, so remote from his traditional haunts, his plays were certainly acted at least as early as 1483, for the same accounts mention that in that year, one Richard Willes was Robin Hood, and collected twenty-three shillings for the church funds. Ten years before, in Norfolk, Sir John Paston arranged for a play or interlude to be given by his servants, and complained in a letter that one of his men had suddenly left him, though, he says, "I have kept him these iii yer to playe seynt Jorge and Robyn Hod and the Sheryf of Notyngham."[1] At Kingston-on-Thames the churchwardens entered the receipts and expenses of the Whitsuntide Kyngham Game and the Robin Hood sports together in 1508 and 1509. The costs included a number of small items, such as food, clothes and payment for the players, "II Kyldyrkenys of III halpeny bere for Robyn Hode and his compeny", 10d. for the hire of a barge, and sums ranging from $\frac{3}{4}$d. to 12d. for "pynnys". The receipts for both "gaderyngs" were four marks in the first year and twenty pence in the second.[2] In 1538 the players at Stratton in Cornwall collected £3 0s. 10d. for the church sums, a large sum for those days and, as those who organize parish whist drives will agree, not inconsiderable for a small village even now.

The popularity of the Robin Hood plays and games was so firmly established in the fifteenth and sixteenth centuries that nothing was allowed to interfere with them. In 1555 the performances were forbidden by Scottish law, but they still continued in spite of the heavy penalties laid down, and when, in 1561, an attempt was made to stop one performance, a serious riot broke out. In a sermon preached before Edward VI in 1549, Bishop Latimer voiced a bitter complaint which shows up clearly the divergences in thought between the stricter shepherds of the newly reformed Church and their conservative flocks. He said:

> I came once myself to a place, riding on a journey homeward from London, and I sent word overnight into the town that I would preach there in the morning because it was holy day, and methought it was an holy day's work. The church stood in my way, and I took my horse and my company and went thither. I thought I should have found a great company in the church, and when I came there, the church door was fast locked.
>
> I tarried there half an hour and more, at last the key was found, and one of the parish comes to me and says: "Sir, this is a busy day with us, we cannot hear you, it is Robin Hood's day. The parish are gone abroad to gather for Robin Hood. I pray you let them not." I was

[1] Paston Letters.
[2] Dr. W. E. Finny, *Mediaeval Games and Gaderyngs at Kingston-on-Thames*.

fain there to give place to Robin Hood; I thought my rochet should
have been regarded, though I were not, but it would not serve, it was
fain to give place to Robin Hood's men.

It is no laughing matter my friends, it is a weeping matter, a heavy
matter, under the pretence of gathering for Robin Hood, a traitor, and
a thief, to put out a preacher, to have his office less esteemed, to prefer
Robin Hood before the ministration of God's word, and all this hath
come of unpreaching prelates. This realm hath been ill provided for,
that it hath had such corrupt judgements in it, to prefer Robin Hood
to God's word.

How clearly the little scene shines across the dividing centuries!
In imagination we can still see the two men standing outside the
empty church in the bright summer morning—the preacher
wounded alike in his religious feelings and his self-esteem, the
embarrassed parishioner, probably a churchwarden, anxious not to
give offence to the powerful minister, but well aware that nothing
short of force would bring the people to church that day. What
consternation must have been felt when the messenger first brought
news of that ill-timed visit; what relief, perhaps faintly tinged
with apprehension, when the disgruntled cleric finally rode
away. To Latimer the incident was just another example of
pagan godlessness and frivolity; to the local men it must have
seemed an unwarrantable interference with a harmless and old-
established custom. We are not told the name of the erring
parish, but it is not important, for probably the Bishop would
have received the same treatment in almost every village in
England, had he been tactless enough to go there on "Robin
Hood's day".

In Maidenhead Thicket is a spot formerly known as Robin
Hood's Bower, a name which occurs in other districts also. It has
been suggested that this was a relic of the real Robin Hood, and
that he, or some other bandit using his name, once infested the
Chiltern Hills. In his day that peaceful and lovely country was
thickly wooded and its inhabitants less law abiding than they now
are; the ancient office of Steward of the Chiltern Hundreds called
for a strong and resolute holder who could control an unruly popu-
lation and maintain the King's peace in the face of difficulties.
The woods and thickets provided ample cover for robbers and

outlaws, and no doubt many took refuge in them from time to time. But no tradition connects Robin Hood or his imitators with this part of England, and in all probability the old place-name commemorated the games played in his honour rather than any incident in his actual life.

The setting up of arbours for the May King and Queen, or for the Lord of Misrule, seems to have been a well-established custom. Stubbes tells us that when the Lord of Misrule was chosen, the people went in procession to the church and danced there, and that afterwards they went

> . . . forth into the church-yard, where they have commonly their summer-halls, their bowers, arbours and banquetting houses set up, wherein they feast, banquet and dance all that day and (peradventure) all the night too.[1]

When Margaret More, of Wistow, was May Queen, about the year 1469, she sat "in the place commonly called the Summer House" from noon till sunset, "making herself agreeable, but with decency."[2] In Cheshire, when the new rushes were brought to the church during the Wakes festival, the rush-cart was surmounted by a bower of greenery in which sat the important individual who directed the proceedings, and this custom persisted in some parishes until the middle of the eighteenth century, when the boarding of church floors reduced the annual rush-bearings from a practical necessity to a mere picturesque survival.

Similar arbours were built for Robin Hood and Maid Marion where their games were played. In 1566 the churchwardens of St. Helen's, Abingdon, paid eighteenpence for setting up Robin Hood's Bower. This would presumably be built in or near the town, for the May and Whitsun games were usually held in some central spot such as the village green or a convenient meadow or common just outside. The churchyard was a favourite spot, as it was also at one time for fairs and markets, and, indeed, for almost every communal celebration. Plays, not necessarily religious in character, were sometimes acted inside the church itself, and

---

[1] Philip Stubbes, *The Anatomie of Abuses*, 1583.
[2] *Testamenta Ebor* (Surtees Society), quoted by S. O. Addy in *Church and Manor*.

dancing in or before the building was not unknown. The church-warden's accounts for St. Edmund's, Salisbury, mention sums received for the church funds from such dances in the early seventeenth century. During the Grovely ceremonies on May 29th the people of Wishford annually danced before Salisbury Cathedral with oaken boughs in their hands, and this practice was continued until a very late date. Grace Read, who was the last person to remember dancing there in her youth, died as recently as 1871. Margaret More's "summer house" was set up in John Dodham's barn, which adjoined the churchyard, and there, according to the evidence given before the York Ecclesiastical Court, the May-games had been held for several years in succession.

In a few parishes, however, the people went out to more distant places and danced and built their bowers on the downs, or by some ancient stone circle. Stow relates in his *Survey of London* how, in 1516, Henry VIII and Queen Katherine went a-maying on Shooter's Hill and were met by a band of young men dressed in green and armed with bows and arrows, who called themselves Robin Hood and his followers. These first displayed their skill in archery, two hundred shooting together with arrows that whistled as they flew, "so that the noise was strange and loud, which greatly delighted the king, queen and their company." They then led the royal party into the woods, "where, in harbours made of boughs and decked with flowers, they were set and served plentifully with venison and wine by Robin Hoode and his men, to their great contentment." This was a summer game on the grand scale, which few villages could hope to imitate, but simpler bowers would doubtless be built occasionally in other woods, where the time-honoured plays were acted in the glades. One such may have been set up in Maidenhead Thicket, and thus preserved Robin Hood's name for a time in a district with which he seems to have had no other association.

The place-names of Nottinghamshire and Yorkshire are in a different category, for here they commemorate the man himself and are attached to places that he must have seen many times during his life. A stone in Sherwood Forest, near Oxton, is called Robin Hood's Pot; an old tree in Birklands, near the Major Oak, is known as his Larder. The Leen rises near Robin Hood's Hills, and on the banks of the Maun is a well-concealed cave where he is said to have hidden on occasion from his pursuers. We cannot now be certain whether he ever did so, but he must have known the place well, for it stands near the ford at Conjure Alders, anciently known as Cunniggeswath, or King's Ford, where the perambulations of the forest used to begin. In the old church at Edwinstowe he is supposed to have married Maid Marion; at Blidworth is the grave of his henchman, Will Scarlet, or Scadlock.

Friar Tuck's cell stood at Copmanhurst in the woods of Fountain Dale, on the banks of the little River Rain. The stones composing it were only removed for agricultural purposes in the middle of last century. Fountains Abbey, in Yorkshire, also claims to be the place where Robin Hood met this redoubtable cleric and was thrown into the water, and at one time the outlaw's bow was kept there and shown to visitors. But there seems to be no evidence that Friar Tuck ever lived in the abbey. His habit of life was more that of a hermit than a monk. He wore a sword and buckler and a cap of steel on his head. He kept a pack of savage dogs to protect him, and trained them to catch arrows in their mouths, so that no one could overcome them until Little John adopted the stratagem of shooting two arrows at once, and so slew fifty of them in one encounter. The ballad of "Robin Hood and the Curtall Friar" says that the latter lived at Fountains Abbey, but it also mentions "Fountains Dale", and it seems likely that the remote spot in the Nottinghamshire woods became confused with the better known abbey in the North. The monks would certainly be tempted to foster the confusion, for any connexion with the outlaw hero was a source of interest and would encourage the lucrative visits of pilgrims to the monastery.

At Robin Hood's or St. Anne's Well, in Nottingham, the hero's cap, chair, slipper and bow were once kept. In the seventeenth and eighteenth centuries it was the custom for visitors to sit in the chair and be formally crowned with the cap. This last, if it ever belonged to Robin Hood, must have been worn out long before Brome wore it on the occasion he described in *Travels Over England*, published in 1700, even if the more durable chair and bow were still in existence. Such things, however, would be a source of revenue to the well-keeper, and no doubt they were religiously renewed when necessary, like John of Gaunt's horse-shoe in the streets of Lancaster. Stevenson tells us that in the early nineteenth century an officer bought Robin Hood's belt and bottle from the custodian, but when a comedian wished to do the same thing later, another was produced for him, and the writer adds that when a boy he "heard the lady at the well declare she could procure another when wanted."[1]

This is not the only well which bears the outlaw's name. Lord Carlisle built a stone arch over the spring so called on the road between Bourwallis and Skelbrough, and here, in coaching days, passengers going north from Doncaster sometimes stopped to drink the water. There is a Robin Hood's Well in Sherwood Forest, near Beauvale Hall, and another on the south bank of the River Skell, by the ruins of Fountains Abbey. His well at Wakefield had a sinister reputation quite unconnected with him, and probably much older than its name, for it was supposed to be the haunt of a barguest, or padfoot, known as the Boggart of Longar Hede. This spectral hound had horns, long shaggy hair, the usual saucer eyes, and a chain on one hind leg. It was followed by a sound like a pack of hounds in full cry, and was regarded as a death omen by all who met it.

Yorkshire's most interesting relic of the robber chief is, of course, his grave. In a letter published in *The Antiquary* for September 1906, Mr. H. Lowerison relates how he visited the farm in June of that year and saw not only the grave itself, but also the chamber in which the hero died. He writes:

The Room was . . . hung with sides of bacon and is known as the bacon-room to the people of Kirklees Priory Farm. It is an upper room of a finely timbered lodge, of the early sixteenth century, perhaps, and is approached by an outer stone stair. On an exterior beam in the gable, not the bargeboard, is a carving of a hunting subject. The farm buildings are quite evidently the remains of the Priory, and just outside the gate are a series of fishponds. From the farmyard another gate leads to the graves—enclosed like Robin Hood's by a tall iron rail—of a former prioress and a little child. From the window . . . the arrow marking the position of the grave is said to have been shot, and the

[1] W. H. Stevenson, *Notes about Nottinghamshire.*

lassie who conducted me gravely pointed out the broken pane. Robin Hood's grave stands in a thicket, perhaps five hundred yards from the lodge.

Legend has buried Little John in three different places—at Hathersage, which can at least claim to be in a district known to the living robber, in Dublin, and in Scotland. The Irish tradition is very vague and seems to rest chiefly on Holinshed's account of a brief visit paid to Dublin by Little John and the recorded execution for robbery of a man, perhaps a player or an imitator, who bore that name. In his *Chronicle* Holinshed says that after the death of Robin Hood, Little John fled to Dublin and remained there for a few days until he was obliged to seek greater security in Scotland, where he died. Before he left, however, he shot an arrow from Dublin Bridge to Osmanstown Green, and a hillock in the latter place was once known as Little John's Shot in memory of this feat. There seems to be no other evidence for his presence in Ireland, and none at all for his death and burial there, since Holinshed states clearly that he "fled into Scotland, where he died at a towne or village called Moravie." This is presumably the place mentioned by John Bellenden more than forty years before Holinshed wrote. He says that Little John's grave was at Pette, in Morayshire, and that:

> He has bene fourtene fut of hycht, with square membris effering thereto. VI.yeris afore the coming of this werk to lycht (i.e. in 1535) we saw his haunch-bane, als meikill as the haill bane of ane man, for we schot our arme in the mouth thairof. Be quhilk apperis how strang and square pepill grew in our regioun afore they were effeminat with lust and intemperance of mouth.[1]

Who this giant was we do not know, but Bellenden is clearly allowing national pride to mislead him when he includes him amongst the people who once "grew in our regioun", for if the bones were really Little John's, it cannot be denied that they were those of an Englishman.

Nothing seems to have impressed the legend-makers so deeply as Robin Hood's skill in archery. He is said to have been able to shoot an arrow a mile or more, and to have spent much time and

---

[1] *Historie of Scotland translatit be maister Johne Bellenden*, 1536.

energy in training his followers to a similar proficiency. Several tumuli in different parts of the country go by the name of Robin Hood's Butts, and are supposed to have been used by him for archery practice. In Cheshire, Robin Hood's Barrow near Tilston Fearnall is pointed out as the mound on which he used to stand when shooting at Beeston Crag, the great castle-topped rock which lies dead ahead of the barrow. We have already seen how, in his dying moments at Kirklees, he struggled from his death-bed to shoot for the last time through the window and so fix the place of his burial. His refuge at Robin Hood's Bay is said to have been chosen in the same way. At one period of his life he was hard pressed by his enemies and forced to leave his usual haunts in Sherwood and Barnesdale Forests. He retreated northwards across the moors, and having gained the coast in safety he stood on Stoupe Brow Beacon and loosed an arrow with the intention of settling wherever it fell—or so local legend insists. It is possible that his method of choice in so vital a matter was actually a little less haphazard. In his *History of Whitby and Whitby Abbey* Lionel Charlton says that at this time

> . . . he always had in readiness, near at hand, some small fishing vessels, to which he could have refuge, if he found himself pursued; for in these, putting off to sea, he looked upon himself as quite secure and held the whole power of the English nation at defiance. The chief place of his resort at these times, where his boats were generally laid up, was about six miles from Whitby, to which he communicated his name, and which is still called Robin Hood's Bay. There he frequently went a-fishing in the summer season, even when an enemy approached to annoy him; and not far from that place he had butts or marks set up, where he used to exercise his men in shooting with the long-bow.

These "butts" were locally supposed to have been built by Robin's orders, but, in fact, they were two small barrows which stood on the moor behind the village. In 1771 their true nature was proved by excavation, and prehistoric remains were found within them. Charlton mentions this discovery in his book, but adds: "However that may be, there is no doubt, but Robin made use of those houses or butts when he was disposed to exercise his men, and wanted to train them up in hitting a mark."

At Whitby Lathes two stone pillars beside the lane leading to Stainsacre commemorated another remarkable feat in marksmanship on the part of Robin Hood and Little John. Tradition says that the two outlaws went to Whitby Abbey to dine with Abbot Richard, who was apparently not included in Robin's usual hatred of the clergy. Their host invited them to show their skill in archery, and each shot an arrow from the top of the monastery. Robin's alighted on the north side of the land; Little John's fell on the south side, about a hundred yards farther on. The distance was about a mile and a half, and the abbot was not unreasonably impressed. He caused two pillars of stone to be set up on the spots where the arrows fell, one 4 ft. high and about a foot square for Robin Hood, and another $2\frac{1}{2}$ ft. high for Little John. The fields on the north and south sides of the lane were called Robin Hood's Close and Little John's Close respectively, and they are so named in eighteenth-century deeds relating to the property.

Incredible as these tales of archery may sound, they can at least be construed as mere exaggerations of a genuine skill. But Robin Hood has other legends which place him definitely in the ranks of the ancient giants. A rock in the River Tame, near Arden Mill, in Cheshire, bears certain markings which are supposed to be the prints of his fingers. He stood on the top of Werneth Low, perhaps on the barrow which once crowned the hill but has now disappeared, and hurled the stone towards the Cheshire Plain. The reason for his action is not recorded, but it is noteworthy that he was not the only traditional stone-thrower of the district. Giants formerly infested the neighbourhood. One lived in a castle near the site of Arden Hall and spent much of his time hurling rocks at another giant who lived in Stockport. Eventually he issued from his stronghold and, in one final titantic contest, destroyed his enemy for ever. What became of him we do not know, but clearly Robin Hood has here inherited some of his attributes, as well as the markings on the rock which, in an earlier period, would undoubtedly have been ascribed to the now almost forgotten giant rather than to any normal human being.

On Brown Down, near Chard, in Somerset, two barrows went by the name of Robin Hood's Butts, but local tradition did not connect them with the usual archery practice. They were said to have been used by Little John and his master for playing quoits, and a small shallow hollow on the top of each barrow was supposed to have been made by the falling quoits. The heroes stood one on each mound and tossed the rings to one another over the not inconsiderable distance of a quarter of a mile. But the most remarkable story of Robin Hood's abnormal strength concerns the immense mass of rock, several tons in weight, which is known as Robin Hood's Penistone. This lies near Halifax, in the corner of a field beside the road between Nettlepot and Wemmergill. The outlaw and his men were amusing themselves one day on the top of Shacklesborough, and Robin picked up the Penistone, balanced it on his right foot, swung it backwards and forwards once or twice, and then kicked it towards Lunesdale. It broke as it flew through the air; part fell in Kelton, and the rest landed in Sleight's Pasture, where it has remained ever since. Another heavy rock in the same district is supposed to have been tossed off his spade when he was digging on a neighbouring hill.

Proverbs concerning Robin Hood or his men are now seldom, if ever, heard, but in the seventeenth century they seem to have been well known. Dr. Fuller says that "Many men talk of Robin Hood that never shot in his bow" was originally a Nottinghamshire saying, but afterwards became general. It means, he tells us, "Many discourse (or prate rather) of matters wherein they have no skill or experience." Another proverb current in his day was "To sell Robin Hood's pennyworths", meaning to sell goods at a price far below their worth. Since the outlaw's wares were usually stolen in the first place, he could afford to sell them cheaply, and in *Robin Hood and the Potter* we see him selling fivepenny pots for threepence and giving away the last five to the Sheriff's wife. It is true that in this instance he subsequently paid their real owner what he asked for them, but that was only after he had robbed the unfortunate Sheriff of his horse and other goods, and so made a handsome profit on the whole day's work. "To overshoot Robin Hood" presumably referred to a highly spectacular, if not impossible, achievement, and "to go round by Robin Hood's barn" meant going the longest way. Camden mentions "Tales of Robin Hood are good for fools", which must have been the sceptic's motto at that period, when the hero's fame was still at its height.

These sayings are no longer part of our current speech, but Robin Hood's Wind still blows in north-east Cheshire and Yorkshire under its old name. It is the bitterly cold wind that ushers in the thaw after a long hard frost, and in the two counties where it is so called, it is said to have been the one discomfort which, for all his hardihood, Robin Hood could not stand.

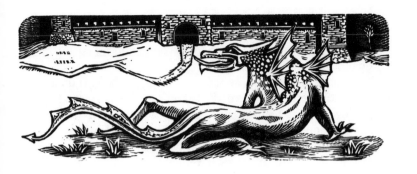

CHAPTER VII

ST. GEORGE

THE patron saint of England differs from those of Ireland and Wales inasmuch as he was not a native of these islands and had no connexion in life with the country that was afterwards to fight proudly under his banner. It was not he who brought Christianity to the English, as St. Patrick did to Ireland; unlike St. Alban, his martyred blood was not spilt on our soil, and no British church or village contained his bones. Although his story was certainly known here as early as the time of the Venerable Bede and may possibly have been introduced through the influence of Gregory the Great, who is said to have felt a strong devotion to him, his cult did not become widespread in England until the period of the Crusades. From then on it was embraced with enthusiasm, and St. George became not only the patron saint of the country, but also a folk-hero whose legend was constantly told or acted by people of all ranks, along with those of Robin Hood and other renowned leaders. His fame overshadowed that of the native saints, like St. Edmund, St. Oswald or St. Dunstan, who were intimately connected with the people for whom they fought or worked; his popularity dimmed even that of St. Thomas à Becket. Like Arthur, he came in time to stand for all that was best in the ideals of chivalry, and even to-day he still remains for us the type of the true soldier-saint, a man distinguished equally by Christian fervour, high moral integrity, and dauntless physical courage.

St. George has perhaps suffered more from the enthusiasm of his past admirers than from the attacks of his detractors. The latter have sought to identify him with an Arian Archbishop of more than doubtful character, who was murdered by an enraged mob in the reign of Julian the Apostate. But this theory carries within it the seeds of its own refutation, and the marvellous legends repeated by his devotees in this and other countries have done far more to obscure the whole question of his historicity and claims to reverence than anything that Calvin, Reynolds or Gibbon ever wrote. The Christian saint has become the centre of an ancient heathen myth; he has been enrolled in the ranks of the dragon-slayers with Perseus, Siegfried, Sigurd and other pagan heroes, and he has been made the chief figure of the death-and-resurrection plays of the Spring Festival. The story of his miraculous escapes from death and his revival by St. Michael made him eminently suitable for this role, and he still appears from time to time in the surviving Mumming plays, either under his own name or its later, corrupted form of "King George".

He is included amongst the saints of the Church by right of his martyrdom during the Diocletian persecutions in the early fourth century. For some time before these began, Christianity had been tolerated in the Roman Empire and included in its ranks many influential and highly placed people, amongst them Diocletian's own wife and daughter. Churches were numerous, and services were freely attended; pagans and Christians intermarried, and the latter seem to have suffered no disabilities on account of their faith. Nevertheless, there were certain undercurrents of dissatisfaction. Complaints were sometimes made by officials against Christians whose ideas seemed to their superiors to lead them into unorthodox, if not actually subversive paths. At the end of the third century some soldiers were executed for breaches of discipline, supposed to be connected with their religion. The discovery of a plot against Galerius, in which Christians were alleged to be involved, eventually fanned the smouldering embers of hostility to a blaze. All soldiers were ordered to sacrifice to the gods without regard to their professed creed; on February 23rd, A.D. 303, the Praetorian Guard raided the Cathedral of Nicomedia without warning, and after conducting a thorough search and burning the scriptures they destroyed the building. On the following day an edict was issued, ordering the destruction of all churches and sacred writings, forbidding meetings for the purposes of worship, and depriving Christians who held office of their rank and citizenship.

This edict seems to have come as a complete surprise to the unfortunate people against whom it was directed. It was followed by a fierce wave of persecution which engulfed even the far-away province of Britain. Churches and books were ruthlessly destroyed and many devout Christians were martyred, including our own St. Alban, Aaron, and Julius of Caerleon. Amongst the first to suffer for their faith was the man who is usually identified with St. George. Eusebius, Bishop of Caesarea, records that as soon as the decree was published in Nicomedia a certain man of high rank boldly tore it down and destroyed it before all the people. His action was the more courageous since two of the Caesars, the first and fourth in imperial rank, were in the city at the time, and he could not, therefore, hope to escape immediate arrest. Eusebius does not tell us his name, but only that he was the first to perish in that district and that he bore torture, imprisonment and death with a calm and serene mind. He is said to have been a soldier and to have followed up his destruction of the edict by going in full armour to the Temple of Bacchus and throwing down the statue of the god. For this and his subsequent refusals to offer sacrifice he was tortured and finally martyred on a date usually supposed to have been April 23rd, A.D. 303.

Little else is known for certain about the man who was afterwards to be venerated throughout Europe and south-western Asia as St. George. He is said to have been a native of Cappadocia, the child of wealthy Christian parents. Early writers agree in describing him as a man of some standing, and it seems probable that he was an officer of fairly high rank in the Roman army. In the Greek Church he is sometimes called Nestor, and this may have been his true name. An ancient panegyric of St. Demetrius found at Pergamos at the end of the nineteenth century calls him Nestor, and also refers to him as The Victor, a title frequently given to St. George in the Greek services. St. Demetrius also suffered martyrdom under Diocletian, and tradition says that the two saints were friends. In the Eastern Church they were closely associated; their churches were built near each other and they appear together on a number of old seals found in Asia Minor and elsewhere. St. George is supposed to have been buried at Lydda at his own request, and in this city his cult afterwards became very strong. A great church was raised over his tomb, and in the eighth century Adamnan, writing of the holy places of Christianity, mentions a marble statue of the saint which had been described to him by Arculfus, a French cleric who had visited Lydda and was later wrecked on the English coast, where he became Adamnan's guest for a time.

Edward Gibbon, in his *Decline and Fall of the Roman Empire*, gives a totally different account of St. George. He asserts that he was not, in fact, a Roman soldier, or even an orthodox Christian, but an army contractor who eventually became the Arian Archbishop of Alexandria. This man was born of poor parents at Epiphania, in Cilicia. He was ambitious and determined at all costs to be rich, and in due course he rose to be a purveyor of provisions to the army in Constantinople. By fraud and graft he became extremely wealthy, but his peculations were detected at last, and he was forced to leave the country very hurriedly and take refuge in Cappadocia. He was not, however, without powerful friends. He had become a convert to Arianism, that dangerous and widespread heresy which denied the equality of Christ with God the Father and at one time threatened to undermine the entire Christian Church by the rapidity with which it grew. His co-religionists not only protected him from the consequences of his misdeeds, but chose him to be their Archbishop in Alexandria, in opposition to St. Athanasius, who was the nominee of the Church. This startling change in his status produced no corresponding alteration in his character. He continued to put his own enrichment before all other interests, and to this end plundered the pagan temples and taxed pagans and Christians alike so unmercifully that he earned the hatred of both parties. When he fell from power on the accession of Julian the Apostate, the oppressed people took their revenge. They broke into the prison where he and two of his accomplices were confined and murdered all three, after which they paraded the bodies through the streets and then threw them into the sea. The Arians, disregarding the provocation received, chose to consider the dead prelate as the victim of pagan religious hatred. To them he was a martyr, and Gibbon asserts that it is from this sect that we have inherited the Christian St. George. "This odious stranger," he says, "disguising every circumstance of time and place, assumed the mask of a martyr, a saint and a Christian hero; and the infamous George of Cappadocia has been transformed into the renowned St. George of England, the patron of arms, of chivalry, and of the Garter."

To this theory of the saint's identity, there are two serious objections. The first is the bitter hatred which existed between Arians and orthodox Christians, a hatred which makes it practically impossible that anyone venerated by the former should be canonized by the latter. St. Athanasius did not suffer the Arian prelate's rivalry in silence; his writings were widely read, and his remarks on the ex-contractor can have left no doubt about the true facts of the case in the mind of any responsible official of the Church. Nor was the Archbishop's own character likely to endear him to those who could not read; in Alexandria, certainly, where he was best known, there was little likelihood of a spontaneous and unofficial veneration such as was given in later times to Simon de Montfort or Henry VI. One cannot help feeling that the Arian leaders must have been actuated mainly by motives of expediency when depicting such a man as a saint and a martyr to their cause. An even more serious objection is provided by the date of his death. He was murdered in A.D. 362 and cannot, therefore, have been regarded as a martyr by anyone before that date. But in the nineteenth century Burkhardt discovered dedications to St. George dating from fifteen or sixteen years earlier. There was a church at Shaka built in his honour about A.D. 346, and another of about the same date at Ezra, in Syria, the inscription of which stated that it contained "the cherished relic of the glorious Victor, the holy Martyr George". At this period the Alexandrian Archbishop was definitely alive and cannot, therefore, be the saint intended.

St. George the Martyr was clearly known to the Eastern Church during the prelate's lifetime, and this, combined with the extreme improbability of the metamorphosis suggested by Gibbon, seems to dispose finally of the claims made on his behalf.

The fame of George-Nestor spread very rapidly through southern Europe and the adjacent Asiatic countries. Numerous churches were dedicated to him, and at least two of these, as we have seen, were built only forty-three years after his death. In Lydda, which claimed to be the place both of his birth and his burial, he was venerated as a local saint, and from thence his cult spread to many other districts. Justinian built a church for him at Bizani, in Armenia; in Rome his head was preserved at an early date and was rediscovered, after being lost, in A.D. 751. He was honoured as a martyr by both Western and Eastern Churches, and became the special guardian of the Byzantine Empire. St. Gregory of Tours records miracles wrought in Gaul through his intercession in the sixth century; his arm was kept in a convent at Barala dedicated to him by Clovis II, and there were other relics in Paris. In England his earliest known church was at Fordington and was mentioned by Alfred the Great in his will, but his story was certainly known here before that time, for the Venerable Bede included him in his list of martyrs a century before and gave April 23rd as his Feast-day. Canute dedicated a monastery to him at Thetford, and in A.D. 1002 Aelfric wrote a metrical *Life of St. George*, in which he is pleasantly described as:

> A rich ealdorman
> Under the fierce Caesar Dacianus
> In the shire of Cappadocia.

St. George's story, or a semi-fabulous version of it, was recorded in the Greek *Acts* of the sixth century, quoted by the Bollandists, and in the Latin *Acts*, which appeared in the eighth century but were supposed to have been compiled by his servant, Pasikras, who was a witness of his martyrdom. Both laid great stress upon the tortures he endured and his miraculous escapes from death, and they provided the foundation for most of the legends subsequently told about him. The sufferings and miracles of the early Christian martyrs were frequently described in accounts known as *Acts* or

Passions, and these were sometimes read in the churches on their anniversaries. They were originally based upon official reports of trials, or the evidence of eye-witnesses, but since every detail known or rumoured about the martyr was carefully collected they inevitably included much that was marvellous and impossible. Like other heroes, the saints inherited incidents from one another, or from legends of paganism. The terrible death of St. Hippolytus was precisely the same as that of the pagan Theseus; the gentle St. Bride of Ireland had many of the characteristics of her predecessor in the same country, the heathen goddess Bride, who was the daughter of the Dagda. Popular traditions or purely fictitious stories were often incorporated in the *Acts* of the martyrs, and these embroideries presented no difficulties to the majority of those who heard or read them, but served rather to make the histories more acceptable and their central figure more greatly loved.

In his *Passions* and in later legends St. George is represented as having suffered untold tortures for periods varying from seven days to seven years. His body was broken on a wheel and restored to life by St. Michael Archangel. He was transfixed by spears, crushed with heavy stones, buried in a cave, thrown into a well, and burnt by molten lead. He was hurled over a precipice in an iron box set with sharp nails, and roasted over a slow fire inside a brazen bull. His feet were shod with shoes of red-hot iron; he was cast into a pit of quicklime, beaten with sledge-hammers and forced to drink poison, as well as a draught intended to destroy his reason. From all of these ordeals he emerged unscathed, not only alive but perfectly whole. His broken limbs were restored to their original state; the marks of burns and scourgings disappeared as soon as the punishment was ended, and all his wounds were immediately healed. Only when God permitted it were his tormentors able to kill him, and they were given no time in which to enjoy their triumph. At the moment of his death his chief enemies were struck by lightning or, according to one version, swept away by a fiery whirlwind.

Like the Seven Sleepers of Ephesus, St. George also figures in Mohammedan legend. Ghergis, or El Khoudi, lived in the time of the Prophet and was sent by God to convert a certain pagan king. Three times the obstinate monarch put him to death, and each time he was restored to life and returned to preach again. On the third occasion his dead body was burnt and his ashes thrown into the river, but God revived him and sent him to destroy the king and all his people. In *Sinae and Palestine* Dean Stanley relates how he saw near Sarafend an empty chapel or sepulchre dedicated to El Khoudi. It contained no tomb, but only hangings before a recess. The local people told him there was no grave within because El Khoudi had never died. He still flies round and round the world, and every now and then reveals himself to its inhabitants. Such chapels were built in the places where he had appeared.

It is not, however, by these early religious legends that St. George is now chiefly remembered, but by the famous story of his fight with the dragon. We do not know definitely when this universal myth was first associated with the warrior saint, but it certainly formed part of his legend by the twelfth century, for not only was it included then in a Prologue to his *Passion*, but it was depicted on a roughly carved tombstone of the same period in Conisborough parish church. In the following century the story was told again, with some differences of detail, by Jacques de Voragine in the *Golden Legend*. In the Prologue version there is no battle; the dragon is overcome simply by the sign of the Cross and is then led back to the city by a strand of the princess's hair. In the *Golden Legend* we have the more familiar tale which includes a fight, the outcome of which depends less upon the miraculous element and more upon the saint's own courage and skill. Silene, a city of Lybia, was troubled by a monster which lived in a lake outside the walls and devoured many of the inhabitants. Its breath poisoned all who approached it, and it easily routed the armed forces sent against it. The unhappy people at first stayed its appetite by giving it two sheep every day, but when the flocks were exhausted it was agreed that one of the citizens should be chosen daily by lot and sacrificed to save his fellows. Eventually the lot fell upon the King's daughter, and though her father offered all his treasure to redeem her, the people insisted that she must suffer with the rest. Eight days' grace was the sole concession made to her youth and royal blood; at the end of that time she was led to the lake-side and left to await the dragon's coming.

St. George: Hero of England

111

There St. George found her and inquired the cause of her tears. She besought him to save himself while there was yet time, but he refused, and prepared to defend her. When the dragon appeared he first invoked God's aid and then attacked the monster, finally overcoming it after a fierce fight, but without killing it. The princess's girdle was passed round its body and by this slender cord she led it back in triumph to Silene. At the sight of their still living enemy the people fled, but they were reassured by the victorious saint, who first converted and baptized them all and then cut off the dragon's head.

This is the legend which occurs again and again in various forms in pagan and Christian tradition. The story which most closely approximates to that of St. George is the legend of Perseus who slew the sea-monster by the power of the Gorgon's head and rescued the captive Andromeda. But it is not the only tale of its kind, even in Grecian mythology. Hercules defeated the Hydra; Theseus killed the dreaded Minotaur who demanded an annual tribute of young human lives. The *Rig-Veda* relates that the blessing of rain was obtained for the parched world by Indra's fight with the serpent, Ahi. In Persia the divine Mithra overcame Ahriman and bound him for three thousand years, and the human Thraetana defeated Dahak, who had three heads and six throats and was endowed with a thousand strengths. Similar stories were told in northern Europe. Fafnir was overcome by the hero Sigurd, and a treasure-guarding monster by Siegfried; Gull-Thorir fought with a winged and scaled dragon of the true fairy-tale order, and Grettir waged a desperate battle under a burial cairn with the dead king, Karr the Old, who had become a vampire. The Anglo-Saxon hero, Beowulf, fought for two nights with Grendel, who infested a swamp near a town on the North Sea and was apparently unconquerable; on the first night the hero put the monster to flight, on the second he killed him with an enchanted sword.

Much later the same stories were told of lesser men whose fame was mainly local, like the ancestor of the Lambton family in Co. Durham who killed the Lambton Worm in the fourteenth century, or Thomas Venables of Moston who freed that Cheshire township from a man-eating dragon. But when Christianity was young it was often the saints who took the place of the heathen heroes and destroyed the traditional monsters by the power of the Cross as their predeccessors had destroyed them by magic or the help of the gods. St. Romanus is said to have slain a dragon at Rouen in the reign of King Dagobert by miraculously inducing it to enter a specially prepared fire in which it was consumed. St. Martial freed Bordeaux from another of these pests, and St. Martha killed the Tarasque of the Rhone whose head, or what was alleged to be its head, was long preserved at Aix. Such legends, despite their universal character, cannot be taken as casting doubt upon the historicity of any particular saint; they were the natural additions made by a wonder-loving people from their own floating traditions, and prove nothing either way. They were, in fact, the religious folk-tales of the time, and were the more easily believed because they were already well known. Moreover, they provided a clear moral lesson, since the dragon obviously represented, or could be made to represent, the powers of evil. St. George's fight and victory were as freely accepted by clergy and laity as the fact of his martyrdom, and though the story was omitted from the office books of the Church when these were reformed by Pope Clement VII, a vernacular version seems to have been read in some churches as late as the end of the fifteenth century. The legend survived the decline of the martyr's cult after the Reformation, and it still remains his distinguishing mark, the first, and sometimes the only, story told about him to the children of our race.

St. George's fame in western Europe spread very widely during the time of the crusades. The vision seen by the Crusaders at Antioch set his name ringing through every country to which the returning warriors could carry it. The Christian army was hard pressed and almost surrounded by the Saracens when they were suddenly heartened by the sight of a mighty host, led by St. George and St. Demetrius, charging down the hill-side to their aid. The whole course of the battle was thus abruptly changed, and victory remained with the Crusaders. Again, during the attack on Jerusalem, the warrior-saint was seen in a blaze of light on the city walls, leading the armies in the assault. Henceforward he was regarded as the special protector of soldiers, and his name became the crusading battle-cry. In Portugal, Aragon, France and England

and throughout the Holy Roman Empire he was the symbol and figurehead of Christian chivalry, and numerous orders of knighthood were founded in his name. One such order was instituted in Aragon in 1201, another in Genoa a few years later. A third was founded by the Emperor Frederick in 1245. Froissart, describing the meeting between the King of Portugal and the Duke of Lancaster in 1387, says that the King was dressed in white robes lined with crimson, with the red cross of St. George upon them, these being the robes of the Order of Avis, of which he was Grand Master. When Robert of Flanders returned from the Holy Land he brought with him relics of the martyr which he presented to Toulouse and to the Abbey of Auchin, and other relics were given to the church of Villars-Saint-Leu in 1101 by a chaplain who had received them from Baldwin in Jerusalem.

We do not know for certain when St. George was first generally accepted as the patron saint of England. He was definitely so styled after the Battle of Agincourt, but long before that time he seems to have been regarded as a specially English saint. In 1191, during the Third Crusade, when Richard I was marching on Acre, his rearguard troops called on the martyr during a desperate engagement and succeeded in driving the attacking Saracens back into the woods from which they had suddenly charged. In 1222 the Synod of Oxford proclaimed his feast to be a general holiday, and thenceforward it steadily grew in popularity. In 1284 the official seal of Lyme Regis showed a ship flying his flag. At the siege of Calais in 1348, Edward III joined St. George's name to that of St. Edward the Confessor in the English battle-cry, and in the following reign every soldier in the Scottish wars was ordered to wear his cross on chest and back. At Agincourt his banner was carried along with that of Our Lady and the Royal Standard; tradition says he appeared in the sky above the English host, and in the ensuing victory celebrations on 23 November 1415 a great statue of the saint in armour was erected on London Bridge. During the same month the Church Council gathered at St. Paul's adjured the faithful of England to pay him special honour as their Patron Saint, and his feast-day was made a double festival, on which none but strictly necessary work might be done.

In 1350 the greatest of the many Orders founded in his name, that of the Garter, was instituted by Edward III. The King himself was its hereditary chief; the members had to be knights of gentle birth and free from all reproach. Froissart tells us that they were "according to report and estimation the most valiant men in Christendom." They met every year on April 23rd in St. George's Chapel, Windsor. This custom was interrupted for a short time in the reign of Edward VI, when the feast-day was abolished as savouring of popery, and the Garter assembly was transferred to another season. The King, who seems to have cherished a particular dislike of St. George, wished to divorce the Order from all connexion with its patron and to omit his name altogether from its title. But Queen Mary restored the ancient customs, and the Knights of the Garter continued from her reign onwards to meet at the appointed time and place. They may still be seen on St. George's Day, in their plumed hats, collars and long mantles, passing in procession down the steps of the chapel, a colourful and beautiful spectacle not unworthy of the mediaeval chivalry from which it springs.

In the fourteenth and fifteenth centuries many of the social and religious Guilds which were so popular in the later Middle Ages were dedicated to St. George. Norwich, Chichester, Coventry, Reading, Leicester and King's Lynn all had guilds of St. George, and there were a few in smaller places, such as Woodbridge, New Romney, and Aston in Warwickshire. At Chester a Guild was founded for the special encouragement of shooting as late as 1537, only a few years before the chill winds of the Reformation blew nearly all these confraternities into oblivion. In Chichester the members were required by their charter to be "respectable citizens", and to attend their annual feast on April 23rd, as well as the mornspeches, or business meetings. They gave a statue of their patron to the Cathedral, maintained a chaplain to say Mass for the souls of their dead, and used their funds to assist both their own brethren, when in need, and other poor people of the city. At King's Lynn the Guild kept five candles burning before St. George's altar on the principal festivals; every member who was in the town at the time was obliged to attend the meetings on pain of being fined, and to behave in seemly fashion thereat, and those who could afford it were expected to buy a livery hood to be worn at mornspeches and burials.

In Leicester a ceremony known as the Riding of the George took place every year, in which not only the members of the Guild, but all the townspeople took part. They were apparently bound to do so, for an Act of Common Hall in 1467 ordered them, upon due summons being made, "to attend upon the mayor to ride against the King,[1] or for riding the George, or any other thing that shall be to the pleasure of the mayor and worship for the town." But probably there were few unwilling citizens, for Throsby in his *History of Leicester* describes the occasion as one of great festivity and rejoicing. It was not always held on April 23rd; the date was fixed by the Master of the Guild and proclaimed at the High Cross and other central places. In the early sixteenth century it seems to have lapsed for a time, for in 1523 the Mayor ordered that the Master of the Guild "should cause the George to be ridden, according to the old ancient custom, that is to say, between St. George's Day and Whit-Sunday, unless there be reasonable cause."[2] The saint himself was certainly represented in the pageant, and there must also have been a dragon, for in the Chamberlain's Accounts for 1536 there is an entry showing that four shillings were paid in that year for "dressing" it.

In Norwich the Fraternity and Guild of St. George was founded in 1348 and granted a charter by Henry V in 1416. Like the other guilds, it gave largely to charity, supported its own members in adversity, and maintained a priest to say Masses for the dead before the high altar in the Cathedral. In 1535 it rented the great hall of the Bishop's Palace for ninety-nine years, and there the annual feast was held on St. George's Day. The George and Margaret procession on the same date was one of the principal events of the Norwich calendar and was so popular that even in the most repressive period of the Reformation it could not be entirely swept away, though it was considerably modified. St. Margaret, who saw the Devil in the form of a dragon, here took the place of the princess who appeared in pageants elsewhere. She and St. George rode in splendid robes of crimson velvet and tawny cloth, on horses caparisoned in black or red velvet ornamented with

[1] i.e. to meet the King. [2] W. Kelly, *Notices of Leicester*.

gold. With them went the dragon whose wickerwork body was covered with glittering scales of gold and green. The Mayor and Aldermen in their scarlet robes accompanied the procession to the Cathedral, which was newly strewn with rushes to receive them, and after the service the parade went out of the city to a wood where, according to an order made in 1408, the legendary fight was re-enacted.

After the Reformation the Guild fell into disfavour because of its religious character, and was only saved from dissolution because it was inextricably mixed up with the City Corporation. It survived until 1732, but long before that time the whole character of the annual procession was altered by the abolition in 1552 of St. George and St. Margaret. The dragon, however, was allowed to remain "for pastime", and for many years thereafter he continued to appear, accompanied by "whifflers" juggling with swords, and men in motley. He was popularly known as Old Snap. In later times the ancient connexion with St. George was still further weakened by the transfer of the celebration from April 23rd to the Tuesday before the Eve of St. John the Baptist. The dragon alone remained as a relic of past glories, and probably few who saw him in the eighteenth century remembered anything very clearly about his origin. Finally he, too, disappeared, after the passing of the Municipal Corporations Act in 1835, which swept away so much that was colourful and interesting in municipal life.

Inn-signs and Mumming plays up and down the country show how widespread and genuine was the cult of St. George in his hey-day. He was not only the patron of military orders and guilds of "respectable citizens"; he was also a hero of the folk who adopted him as the central figure of their village plays and refreshed themselves under his sign at the village inn. In the Mumming plays he was, and still is in some surviving versions, the victorious champion who fights and overcomes his opponent, and sometimes a whole series of opponents. In a Ross variant, collected by Mrs. Leather in 1908, he himself dies after killing several other people, including Napoleon Bonaparte, but this is not usual; in this case the final victor is the Doctor. The Mumming plays almost certainly derive from ancient vegetation rites, and St. George's legend of long imprisonment in a cave and escape therefrom, of death and miraculous resurrection, coupled with the spring date of his martyrdom, made him an obvious hero for such plays. Once he was introduced into them, his place was not disputed. Not every surviving play includes him, but he appears in the great majority, and always as the most prominent character. Very often he is known as King George, an easy corruption in Hanoverian times, sometimes as Prince George, and once simply as Great George, but whatever he is called he remains the central figure. His most usual enemy is the Turkish Knight, who is occasionally styled the Turkish Champion, or the Black Prince of Morocco. This character clearly recalls the Crusades, but there are other opponents, and later wars are commemorated in some versions by Oliver Cromwell, French Officer, Bonaparte, and Edward Vernon. In a few plays the dragon is the enemy, but in most variants he has given place to some human combatant.

St. George nearly always describes himself as "a man of courage bold" and challenges all-comers; in the Ross play he tells his own story in his opening speech, which runs:

> Then in comes I St. George, who did from England spring.
> Oft-times do my wondrous works do fourfold to begin.
> Girt in a closet I was kept
> And then upon a cabin set,
> And then upon a rock of stone,
> When Satan made my body moan;
> I slew the fiery dragon; I beat him to a slaughter,
> And by those means I won the King of Egypt's daughter.
> I fought him off most manfully
> But still came on the victory.
> Where is the man that will against me stand?
> I will cut him down with my courage in hand.

And cut them down he does, one after the other, Prince Valentine, Captain Rover, Turkey Snipe, Little John, Bonaparte and Sambo, until by a most unusual variation in the text of these plays he is himself killed by the Doctor, the descendant of the tribal Medicine Man.

In Puritan times St. George fell into disfavour along with the rest of the saints. In the worst period of intolerance his cult was specially attacked precisely because it had been so popular, and from the battering of that tempest it emerged only in fragmentary form. He was never again to be quite the vivid and living personality that he had been for the ordinary man. Calvin questioned his existence apart from pagan myth, Reynolds and Gibbon confused him with the Arian prelate, the simple actors of Mumming plays confused him with their Hanoverian monarchs. Nevertheless, he survived as something more than a mere mediaeval legend. He remained the Patron Saint of England and of her fighting men; he lived on also as a national hero in the wider sense, whose name still has the power to stir our hearts, like those of Nelson and Drake, and whose virtues are still held up for emulation. His ancient banner is the flag of our country and of our national church; his name meets us constantly in poetry and romance, in the dedications, paintings and windows of old and modern churches, and on the swinging signs of comfortable inns. The youngest of all the churches raised by Englishmen in his honour is one which he would surely have appreciated. It was built by soldiers in the Western Desert during the late war. Its walls and altar were of desert stones, over which the tides of battle had already swept; its cross and candlesticks were made from gun parts, and its bells from empty shell-cases. And there during the desert fighting, in that remote church overlooking a deep wadi, the soldiers of England worshipped, as in bygone ages, under the patronage of England's soldier-saint.

CHAPTER VIII

THE HEROES OF THE CONQUEST

WHEN William, Duke of Normandy, was planning the conquest of England, Halley's comet was visible in our skies and was regarded by many as a portent of evil to come. Change and uncertainty were in the air. Harold Godwinson sat uneasily on the throne to which he had been legally elected by the Witan, but already William had laid claim to the English crown by virtue of Edward the Confessor's alleged promise and the oath extorted from Harold himself when he was a prisoner in Normandy. The end of an era was approaching, and Aethelmaer of Malmesbury was not far wrong when he prophesied that the appearance of "the hairy star" would be followed by the tears of women and the downfall of the kingdom. Between the easy-going Saxon way of life and the harsh rule of a foreign duke stood only Harold and the gallant men who served him; and these, for all their courage and the King's great military skill, were not enough. Harold fell at Hastings with his house-carles round him, and with him the old free life of Saxon England passed away for ever.

These house-carles were the last remnant of the English army to withstand the Norman onslaught. They were their ruler's personal followers, the famous *comitatus* of the Saxon kings, whose tradition demanded that no member should leave a battle-field alive if his lord were killed. In this, the last battle of the old order, that tradition was not broken. Long after Harold himself had fallen and the rest of the English army had been defeated, the house-carles fought on under a hail of arrows till the last man was killed. When the English mourners came to bury their dead, the King's body could not be distinguished from the stripped and mutilated corpses of his men, and here perhaps we see the first beginnings of the subsequent legends of his escape. Tradition says that Edith Swan-Neck, who loved him, searched through the dreadful heaps of dead and dying until she recognized, or thought she recognized, the body of the King, and that it was this corpse which was afterwards demanded from the victor by Queen Githa.

Two contradictory stories are told of Harold's burial. William de Poitiers, the Duke's chaplain, says the Conqueror refused Githa's plea for the restoration of her husband's body, though she offered its weight in gold as a ransom. He declared the dead King to be unworthy of a tomb, since he was an oath-breaker and the cause of many men's deaths, and ordered him to be buried on the sea-shore where he could "guard the coast which he had madly occupied". Ordericus tells us that the body was handed over to William Mallet for interment in an unmarked grave on the beach. Such treatment of a defeated but gallant rival was very unusual, and if William ever gave such an order it is probable that he rescinded it later. The vindictive spirit behind it can only have sprung from his determination, from which he never wavered, to regard himself as the rightful successor to Edward the Confessor and all who opposed him as rebels. How far he really believed in his own claims it is difficult to tell. Edward the Confessor is said to have promised him the succession, or at least to have agreed to use his influence with the Witan to secure it. But if he ever made such a promise he seems to have repented of it later, for on his death-bed he named Earl Harold, and the Witan, in whose hands alone lay the choice of England's kings, accepted the recommendation without hesitation. William's viewpoint, however, enabled him to see his armed conquest of the country as the mere suppression of a rebellion against the rightful king, and in this rebellion

Harold was obviously the arch-offender, who had not only stolen William's throne but had broken his oath to support the Norman claim.

The other story, which is almost certainly the true one, is that the King's body was given to his widow and buried at Waltham. Apart from the fact that a tomb, which has now disappeared, was long pointed out there as Harold's, all the probabilities are against the action ascribed to William by his chaplain. He may indeed have refused Githa's plea in the first flush of victory and threatened to bury her husband in the outlandish manner described by de Poitiers, but it is very improbable that the threat was carried out. To deny the last services of the Church to a christened corpse was a serious matter, and neither as churchman nor king was William likely to do in cold blood anything so grossly shocking to the feelings of his age.

Harold's death was a disaster for the English, for he was the one strong man capable of ruling in that unsettled time and success-fully opposing the invader. His young sons remained, and Edgar the Ætheling, great-nephew of Edward the Confessor, but none of these was of the type to grasp so savage a nettle. It was almost inevitable that rumours should spring up immediately after Hastings that he was not dead, but had escaped, and these were strengthened, if they were not originally started, by the uncer-tainty as to whether the corpse recognized by Edith Swan-Neck was, in fact, that of the King. But they had not the tenacity of similar legends told of other heroes, and they seem to have faded quickly. It is true that Giraldus Cambrensis, two hundred years later, relates a story that Harold was only wounded at Hastings and lived to become a hermit in Chester, and to have a long and secret interview with Henry I before he died. Yet the belief can hardly have been widespread during the first years of William's reign, for when, in 1067, the West and North rebelled against him, they did so, not in the name of their former king, but in that of his young sons at Exeter and of Edgar the Ætheling in the North. Had any real hope survived of Harold's return the insur-gent leaders would have been quick to spread it, for what the English most lacked at that time was a strong man who could serve as a rallying point and unite his countrymen under one powerful and trusted head. That no mention was made of him during the desperate struggles in the West and North, and later in the Fens, is a more clearly written death certificate than any epitaph inscribed upon his tomb.

Nevertheless, if the King was dead, the Saxon resistance was not yet broken, and the first few years of William's reign were marked by a series of uprisings in different parts of England. Among the insurgent leaders there were two who were destined to live not only in the history but also in the folk-lore of their country— Wild Edric and Hereward the Wake. These men came from opposite sides of England, the one from the Welsh Marches, the other from the eastern Fens. Very little is known of their personal history before they revolted, and not much afterwards. Their lineage is uncertain, and even the date and place of their deaths cannot be definitely stated. Yet Edric in his own district and Hereward throughout England are remembered whenever the Conquest is recalled, and the latter especially lives as a patriot hero in the minds of thousands of people who would be hard put to it to name any of the better-known characters of that troubled period.

So thick a mist of legend and fairy-tale has gathered round Wild Edric that it is sometimes difficult to remember that he actually existed. He is recorded in Domesday as the holder of lands in North Herefordshire and Shropshire in the reign of Edward the Confessor. These lands were not in his possession at the time when the Survey was made, nor did they pass to his heirs, but whether he lost them by forfeiture or in some other way is not known. He had the misfortune to be the nephew of Edric Streona, Ealdorman of Mercia, that extraordinary traitor of whom William of Malmesbury says:

> This fellow was the refuse of mankind, the reproach of the English; an abandoned glutton, a cunning miscreant who had become opulent not by nobility but by specious language and impudence. This artful dissembler, capable of feigning anything, was accustomed by pretended fidelity to scent out the king's designs, that he might treacherously divulge them.[1]

He was Ethelred's evil genius and contributed very largely by his

[1] William of Malmesbury, *Gesta Regum*.

advice and influence to that unhappy king's misfortunes; he
betrayed Edmund Ironside and Canute in turn and was suspected
of Edmund's murder; he was finally killed by Canute's order,
"very justly", as the *Anglo-Saxon Chronicle* records. This man of
low birth rose to great power and wealth through Ethelred's
favour, and is one of the very few characters in history for whom
no single chronicler has a good word. The most curious thing
about him is not so much his apparent inability to be loyal to
anyone, as his gift of persuading those he had betrayed to trust
him again to their undoing. "Never was greater folly than that,"
says the writer of the *Anglo-Saxon Chronicle*, when recording his
pardon by Edmund Ironside after his treachery at Sherston;
in the same paragraph the chronicler, describing the Battle of
Ashingdon, relates how "ealdorman Edric did as he had often
done before: he began the flight with the men from the Welsh
border, and so betrayed his king and lord and the whole English
nation."

Such was the best-known member of Wild Edric's immediate
family. No man can justly be blamed for the crimes of his uncle,
and we have no evidence that in this case the nephew was less
highly regarded because of them. But there is one curious difference between his legend and that of Hereward. Both men submitted to the Conqueror when their gallant resistance had finally
failed. No one ever questioned Hereward's action, either then or
later, nor did his reputation as a hero suffer because he had "made
peace". Local tradition was less kindly to Edric. A legend still
current in the late nineteenth century declared that he was unable
to die and was condemned, like the Wandering Jew, to live on
indefinitely because he had given up the fight prematurely. It is
just possible that this singular difference in the traditions of the
two heroes may have been due to his contemporaries' knowledge
of the bad blood that ran in Edric's veins, and a consequent
suspicion that his submission was not so much a necessity as a
first step along the evil road trodden by his uncle before him.

If so, the judgment was probably less than just. Wild Edric
held out for nearly three years, and during that period inflicted
great damage upon the enemy. In the summer of 1067 he made
an alliance with Bleddyn and Rhiwallon, two Welsh princes who

had been Harold's men, and on August 15th their combined forces attacked Herefordshire, ravaging the county as far as the River Lugg and seriously threatening the Norman garrison in Hereford itself. Every force sent against him from Richard's Castle and Hereford was repelled with considerable loss, and two years later he was still fighting. In 1069 he besieged and burnt Shrewsbury with the help of the men of Chester, and then withdrew, still uncaptured, before William's advancing armies. In the following year he seems to have realized that further resistance was hopeless, and at some time between June and August he submitted to the Conqueror. Local tradition has always insisted that he "made peace" as between one ruler and another. He was neither defeated nor captured, and it is perhaps this fact which later gave a flavour of betrayal to what was probably no more than a clear-sighted recognition of the inevitable. He seems to have been received with honour at William's court, and in 1072 we hear of him again as one of those who took part in the King's expedition to Scotland.

What happened to him thereafter is uncertain. When the Domesday Survey was compiled in 1086 his lands had already passed to Ralph de Mortemer and other Normans, which suggests that he may have quarrelled with William at some period subsequent to 1072. One writer[1] alleged that he took up arms against Mortemer and was afterwards condemned to perpetual imprisonment, but for this there is no reliable evidence. Wigmore Castle, which he is said to have defended, was never his, nor was he, as the author calls him, an earl. The date of his death and his burial place are alike unknown, and in this circumstance we may perhaps see the origin of the most famous legend concerning him.

In this he appears as an undying hero who not only lives on till his country's wrongs are righted, but has also assumed many of the attributes of fairies and of the Wild Hunt. Tradition says he never died, but was condemned to haunt the lead-mines of Shropshire with his wife and all his followers. The miners spoke of his band as "the Old Men", and declared that the sound of their underground knocking was the sign of a good lode. Whenever England was threatened by a serious war he rode out over the

---

[1] Sir William Dugdale, *Monasticon Anglicanum*.

surrounding hills, always in the direction of the enemy country.
Miss Burne[1] tells us that he was seen riding south before the
Napoleonic Wars, and again in 1853 or 1854 before the outbreak
of the Crimean War. On that occasion a Rorrington miner and
his daughter saw a band of horsemen sweep by at Minsterley with
Wild Edric and Lady Godda at their head. The father warned the
girl to cover her face and not to utter a sound till all had passed,
otherwise she would go mad, a warning which clearly shows that
the historical hero had become confused with the ancient Wild
Hunt, upon whose divine leader it was dangerous for mortal men
to look. She did as she was told, but what she saw enabled her
afterwards to describe Edric and Godda, and to give certain details
of their appearance which suggest a strong local tradition rather
than the unaided imagination of a young and uneducated girl.
She said that Edric had dark curly hair and black eyes. He wore
a short green coat and cloak, a green cap with a white feather in it,
and a short sword hanging from a golden belt. He was mounted
on a white horse and carried a horn in his hand; it was the sound
of this horn which had first attracted the girl's attention to the
host. Godda was also dressed in green, with a dagger at her waist
and a white linen band round her forehead, on which was a gold
ornament. Her hair, which was golden and wavy, was worn loose.
This was Wild Edric's last recorded appearance as a prophet of
war. No one seems to have seen him in 1914 or 1939, or before
the South African War, so perhaps his punishment is ended. A
lingering tradition still asserts, however, that the lead-miners
always know by some mysterious means when any war is going to
be really serious, and presumably this is because of their close
relation with the "Old Men" of the mines.

Bomere Pool, near Shrewsbury, was formerly supposed to contain a monster fish which wore Wild Edric's sword at its side.
This pool was the subject of several legends concerning a lost
village or city within its depths. Bells were said to ring under its
surface, a Roman soldier's ghost rowed across it on certain widely
spaced dates, and sometimes houses were seen and children were
heard crying in its drowned streets. The monster fish, which was
probably its guardian spirit, could not be caught by any net and

[1] C. S. Burne, *Shropshire Folklore*.

was occasionally seen resting in the shallower parts of the lake with the sword through its belt. This sword it received in trust when Wild Edric disappeared. Tradition says that Condover Hall once belonged to Edric, who was born there, and was later defrauded of it, and only to one of his descendants, the rightful heirs of the property, will the fish render up its charge.

The chief interest of this legend lies in the association of the hero with what is clearly a fairy fish, and the persistence of the belief that he was wrongfully despoiled of his lands. Certainly his heirs never inherited them, nor do we know why this was so. Condover, however, was never his, and it is not very probable that he was born there. The curse which is said to lie on the manor cannot have been laid by him, for he had no interest in the place.[1] Local tradition,[2] nevertheless, asserts that it was, and some sixty years ago his angry ghost is said to have appeared at the hall and repeated the curse in all its details to the horrified owner and his guests.

Yet another legend gives Edric a fairy wife whom he stole from her sisters in the Forest of Clun. The story follows the usual pattern of such tales, in which the wife forbids her husband to say certain words or perform a particular action on pain of losing her. In this case the lady refused to speak at all for three days after her capture. On the fourth day she said she would stay with him, provided he never reproached her on account of her sisters or the place from which she came, that is to say, with her alien origin. This promise he gave, after which they were married and lived happily for many years. Then one day Edric came home to find his wife unaccountably absent. When she returned he accused her of visiting her sisters, whereupon she instantly vanished and was never seen again.

It is not clear whether the fairy wife was the Lady Godda of the lead-mines or another. The names of Edric's real wife and children, if he had any, are not recorded. Walter Map, who included

---

[1] It is possible that legend has confused Condover with Bayston, which touches the shores of Bomere and was once part of Condover parish. Here Edric held lands in the time of Edward the Confessor. Condover itself was royal property before the Conquest.

[2] Another and equally fallacious legend ascribes the curse to a servant who was falsely accused of murder and hanged in the reign of Henry VIII.

this story in *De Nugis Curialium*, refers to a son named Aelfnoth, the child of the fairy, who lived to become a devout churchman and to present the manor of Lydbury North to the Bishopric of Hereford. But the Domesday Book mentions no such landowner, and in any case Lydbury belonged to the bishopric before his time. Walter Map's account also differs from the usual tradition in that he says Edric died of grief when he lost his wife, an event which seems to have occurred many years after his reconciliation with William I.

The last and greatest of the Conquest folk-heroes was Hereward the Wake. Like Wild Edric, he has become the centre of many old-established folk-tales, but his feet were far more firmly set in this world; his death was never denied, and no legend exists of any subsequent return either to warn or to curse his fellow-men. Nevertheless, except for his exploits at Peterborough and Ely, we know hardly anything about him. He appears suddenly, like Arthur, as a full-bown leader, thrown into the limelight of history by a single sentence in the *Anglo-Saxon Chronicle*. That he held lands in Lincolnshire, and possibly also in Warwickshire and Worcestershire, we know from Domesday. Tradition says he was born at Bourne, and it seems probable that he was of Lincolnshire stock. The Abbot of Peterborough was his overlord, and one such abbot, Brand, is usually said to have been his uncle. Of his parents nothing is known for certain; some chronicles give him two wives, others only one. He is variously said to have died peacefully in his bed after submission to William I, or to have been murdered by jealous Norman knights who resented his presence in the Conqueror's expedition to Maine. All that is really certain about him is that he held certain lands mentioned in Domesday, that he sacked Peterborough in 1070, that he afterwards helped to defend Ely for twelve months, and finally escaped with a few of his men when that stronghold fell.

Perhaps the most mysterious thing about him is the manner in which he, a man hitherto unknown to history, assumed command in the Isle of Ely over the heads of far more important people. He seems to have come of good landholding stock, but nothing more; there is no evidence that his family ever ranked amongst the great ones of the land. *De Gestis Herwardi Saxonis* says he was the son of

Leofric and Godiva, and thus the uncle of Edwin and Morcar, but this is almost certainly untrue. Leofric, Abbot of Peterborough, was Earl Leofric's nephew, and Hereward was the abbot's man and also the nephew of the later Abbot Brand; a confusion of these various relationships, together with the constant tendency to ascribe high rank to popular heroes, is perhaps the origin of this legend.

It may be that his pre-eminence as a leader was due to a reputation gained earlier in the struggle at Hastings, for though we do not know for certain that he was there, it seems highly probable. Abbot Leofric certainly was, and died soon afterwards of sickness and grief. Hereward was his man, and both his circumstances and his temperament makes it likely that he followed his lord to that ill-starred fight. Wace tells us in his *Chronicle* that Lincolnshire was one of the counties which sent a contingent of men to Hastings, and if Hereward was in England then it is almost certain that he was one of them. It is true that *De Gestis* says he was in Flanders, having been outlawed earlier at the request of his father, Leofric, but few, if any, of the stories told about him before the sack of Peterborough are trustworthy. Whatever the cause it is clear that he was the mainstay and inspiration of the Ely defence, and some reason there must have been for his unquestioned position there. His name was sufficient to rally to the Isle not only the men of the surrounding districts, but also others from as far away as Berkshire. A number of men from that county, tenants of St. Mary of Abingdon, set out to join him in 1071, but were surprised and defeated by a party of Normans on their way. Of these men we know; not improbably there were others who also made their way from different parts of England to what was the last stronghold of the patriotic movement still active under a man whose courage and initiative were widely known and trusted.

Later chronicles supply a number of details of Hereward's early career. *De Gestis* makes him the son of Leofric and Godiva, and relates how, in his youth, he was so turbulent and wild that his father asked Edward the Confessor to banish him from the country. There is a reference in Domesday to certain lands at Ripinghale held by Hereward from Crowland Abbey which returned to the Abbot because Hereward had fled the country, but it is not at all clear whether this flight occurred after Ely or, as the legends suggest, at some time before the Battle of Hastings. *De Gestis* says he was driven from home with a single follower, one Martin Lightfoot, and sought refuge with his godfather, Gisebert, in Scotland. Here he distinguished himself by killing a ferocious bear which had escaped from Gisebert's private menagerie and was terrorizing the district. The admiration excited by this exploit roused the jealousy of the local men, and he was forced to fly after killing three of them in a fight. He went to Cornwall and was immediately involved in the affairs of a Cornish princess who was betrothed against her will to a champion or giant named Ulcus Ferreus. By defeating this champion, Hereward once again roused the antipathy of the local people, and he went to Ireland, where lived the man whom the princess loved. Here he took part in various wars and, returning with the Irish prince to Cornwall, rescued the princess and restored her to her lover.

The death of his father now recalled him to his estates, but the ship in which he sailed for Lincolnshire was wrecked on the coast of Flanders. After a short imprisonment as a spy, he was honourably received by the Count of Flanders, and fought for him in several expeditions. Here also he married Torfrida. Finally, hearing of the conquest of England, he returned home, and in 1069 arrived at Bourne, where he set fire to three cottages on the highest point of the Brunneswold as a signal to all patriots. To him rallied many Englishmen, and finally this band of heroes repaired to Ely on the invitation of the monks who had already fortified their island under the direction of the loyal Abbot Thurstan.

Historia Croylandensis repeats these legends, some of which are obvious folk-tales, only later applied to a much-admired leader. The fact remains that we know nothing definite of Hereward until 1070. In 1069, Abbot Brand of Peterborough died; "afterwards," says the *Anglo-Saxon Chronicle*, "came all wretchedness and all evil to the minster, God have mercy on it!" At the following Easter Gemot, Turold, a Norman monk, was appointed in his place, a man chosen by William for his severity and his soldierly qualities rather than for his holiness. The Danes were then before Ely; the northern revolt was running to its disastrous close, and already many patriots had made their way to the lonely and swamp-surrounded Isle.

Turold set out for his new dwelling with an armed escort of Normans and was met at Stamford with the news that a mixed band of angry tenants—Danes and Englishmen, which the *Anglo-Saxon Chronicle* calls "Hereward and his gang"—were about to attack the abbey. One Yware, a churchwarden, had hastily collected such books and smaller valuables as he could, and on June 1st sent an appeal for help to Turold. But it was already too late. Early in the morning of June 2nd Hereward's ships appeared in the river. The monks' resistance was quickly overcome and served only to enrage the assailants, who regarded them as traitors to the English cause. The town was set on fire, and the attackers streamed into the monastery through the Bolhithe Gate. They systematically plundered the minster, removing books, money, shrines and every sort of treasure, including the silver pastoral staff which had been hidden in the steeple. The monks, who had made a belated and unsuccessful attempt to placate their enemies when they entered the precincts, now fled, leaving only one sick man, Leofwine Lang, in the infirmary. No one was killed, but when Turold finally arrived with his armed guard he found only this monk, a burnt-out town and a church, itself unharmed, from which every valuable had been stripped.

Hereward withdrew to Ely. Once there he shone out as the natural leader of that desperate band of men, many of whom were of far higher rank than himself. Morcar had escaped from William's court some weeks before and made his way to the Isle; Siward Barn, the Northumberland thegn, was already there, with Aethelwine, Bishop of Durham, and many others. After the Peterborough raid the Danish fleet returned to Denmark, and the English prepared to fight on alone. The Isle itself was eminently defensible, being surrounded by impenetrable morasses and approached only by two or three ancient roads, of which Aldreth Causeway was the most vulnerable. Later in the struggle, Beda, a Norman who had been taken prisoner and subsequently released, described to William the meres and fens which protected the island, and the great natural food supply with which it was endowed.[1] No siege, however long, could starve out the defenders, and the Fen-men, with their local knowledge, could pass freely by means of leaping-poles in places where their enemies could not hope to follow. Abbot Thurstan had been Harold's man and is usually said to have been strongly pro-English; certainly the monks in his charge seem to have sympathized heartily with the revolt, at all events in its early stages. Beda described to his overlord how monks and soldiers sat together in the refectory, with their weapons hanging on the walls round them, so that layman and cleric alike might spring to arms without delay whenever the occasion arose.

In this natural stronghold the English held out for a year. William was forced to use his utmost skill and strategy to dislodge them, and tradition asserts that they were finally defeated, not by superior force, but by treachery. The King concentrated his main attack on the vulnerable point at Aldreth, and began to build a bridge there with trees, hides, and stone brought from Cottenham. The defenders foiled his attempts to enter the Isle by this means on several occasions, and it is round the struggle for the bridge that most of the well-known stories of the siege are centred. Once Hereward disguised himself as one of the fishermen employed by William to carry stores to Aldreth, and succeeded in setting fire to these stores. In the same way he is said to have burnt the wood of the great mounds built by the Normans for the attack. On another day he disguised himself as a potter and went boldly to the royal camp at Brandon, where he sold his wares and escaped unharmed, after killing a soldier and a servant in a fight. When the Normans asked the supposed potter whether he knew Hereward, he replied that he did, to his cost, for the English leader had stolen all his goods except the few pots he had with him.

The most famous story of the defence is that of the witch. Ivo Taillebois is said to have persuaded William to employ her for the encouragement of his own men and the terrorization of his enemies. If William really did consent to this proposal it must have been against his better judgment, for normally he was far too good a churchman to meddle willingly with the powers of evil. The story goes that when Hereward went to Brandon in his

[1] *Liber Eliensis.*

potter's disguise, he lodged in the same house as the witch and heard her plotting his downfall with her hostess. The two women spoke in French (or, according to some versions, in Latin), which they naturally supposed an illiterate Saxon potter would not understand. In the middle of the night they went down to a spring in the garden, and their intended victim heard them "asking responses" of its supernatural guardian. When William began his assault a few days later, the witch was set on a high wooden tower, where all could see and hear her, and there she began to cast spells against the English, a spectacle calculated to strike terror into any man's heart in that age when magic was still a potent and living force.

Hereward, however, was forewarned, and did not wait for her spells to take effect. As she was beginning her third chant the English set fire to the reeds which grew everywhere in that place, and a strong wind carried the flames with great speed towards the Norman position. The startled attackers saw first clouds of smoke and then a wall of fire suddenly sweeping down upon them. The author of De Gestis tells us how:

> Extending some two furlongs, the fire, rushing hither and thither among them, formed a horrible spectacle in the marsh, and the roar of the flames, with the crackling twigs of the brushwood and willows, made a terrible noise. Stupefied and excessively alarmed, the Normans took to flight, each man for himself; but they could not go far through the desert paths of the swamp in that watery road, nor could they keep the path with ease. Wherefore very many of them were suddenly swallowed up and overwhelmed with arrows, for in the fire and in their flight they could not with javelins resist the bands of men who came out cautiously and secretly from the Isle to repel them. And among them that woman aforesaid of infamous art in the great alarm fell down head first from her exalted position and broke her neck.

Many were drowned and many more fell to the English arrows; William himself narrowly escaped death in the confusion and not unnaturally rounded on his advisers, saying that the disaster had been caused solely by the witch and his own folly in listening to the evil counsel of those who wished him to employ her.

So ended the attempt to win by sorcery; fire, that powerful prophylactic against witchcraft, had not only broken the spells but had also routed the soldiery. But what neither magic nor military skill could do, treachery could. Morcar is said by some to have been the traitor, having been promised a pardon if he betrayed his companions. Another and more probable version says that it was the monks themselves who, hearing that William was seizing all their lands outside Ely, secretly offered to show him a way through the defences. Whoever was actually to blame, the fact remains that the Normans appeared suddenly within the Isle, having crossed the Ouse at Aldreth almost without resistance. The gallant defence was ended. The leaders, all but Hereward, surrendered. Morcar, Siward Barn and Aethelwine were imprisoned; the lesser men were punished in various ways. No one was executed, for that was against William's policy, but many suffered the dreadful penalty of having their eyes put out or their hands cut off, and being turned, thus maimed, upon a world in which their enemies were everywhere triumphant. The monastery was fined seven hundred marks and brought to the verge of ruin. Images and treasures had to be melted down to pay this enormous sum, a castle was built within the precincts, and the monks were forced to house and feed a number of Norman soldiers. Thurstan himself was threatened with deposition, but was finally allowed to retain his office until he died, worn out by worry, in 1073.

In these disasters Hereward did not share. Unlike Morcar and the others, he would not surrender, and being warned in time by a monk named Alqyne, he escaped with a few followers to the ships which he kept in readiness, and made for the open sea. Tradition says he returned to a wood near Bourne, and from there harried the lands of nine counties. All the chroniclers agree that he finally made his peace with William and received back at least some of his estates. They do not agree as to his end. Ingulf says that:

> . . . after great battles and a thousand dangers frequently braved and nobly terminated, as well against the king of England as against his earls, barons, prefects, and presidents, which are yet sung in our streets; and after having fully avenged his mother's wrongs with his own powerful right hand, he obtained the king's pardon and his paternal inheritance, and so ended his days in peace, and was very lately buried with his wife nigh to our monastery.[1]

[1] *Historia Croylandensis*. Bohn's ed. 1854.

The wife here referred to is Torfrida. According to some versions of Hereward's story she left him to become a nun, and he subsequently married Alftruda, or Aelfthryth, who, after the fall of Ely, made her own peace with the King and obtained a pardon for her husband.

In *L'Estorie des Engles* Gaimar gives a different account of Hereward's end. He says that after his reconciliation with William he took part in the latter's expedition to Maine. There is an air of probability about this, for it was the King's custom, whenever possible to employ on foreign expeditions the men whose power and influence he had reason to fear at home. Gaimar says that the reconciliation between the two men was genuine, and the Conqueror, who admired courage when he met it, was well disposed towards Hereward. But others were jealous, and their threatening attitude forced him to have guards continually about him within and without the house, and particularly when he sat at meat. On one occasion Aethelward, his chaplain, slept at his post when on guard, and a band of Normans broke into the room where Hereward was. He fought till his sword and spear were both broken, and he was obliged to use his shield as a weapon. Fifteen Normans were killed in the struggle. Finally Hereward was forced to his knees. Ralph of Dol, a Breton, struck him a fatal blow, but, making a last effort, he killed his assailant with his buckler, and the two men fell dead together. Then Asselin, one of the attackers, cut off his head and swore by God and His might that he had never seen so valiant a man. Had there been three more like him, he said, the Normans would never have conquered England.

We cannot now be certain which of these versions is correct, or whether the truth lies in some other and unrecorded direction. But there is no doubt which of the two deaths ascribed to him Hereward himself would have preferred. His character shines out clearly across the intervening centuries and all the conflicting legends which have at once obscured and heightened his fame. "A noble man, one of the best of his country," says Gaimar— brave, great-hearted, boisterous, a man difficult to control but easy to trust—such a man would have hated to die tamely in his bed, and for his sake one can but hope that Gaimar's version is true.

With his submission the English resistance to the Conquest ended, and the long, slow work of welding Norman and Saxon into one nation began; but through all the changes that were to follow, down to the present day, Hereward remained and still remains a hero of the folk and one of the glowing lights of our national tradition.

CHAPTER IX

KINGS AND SAINTS

WHEN St. Augustine landed on the shores of England in
A.D. 597, he found a country which had once been partly
Christian and where Christianity, though almost obliterated by Saxon paganism, still lingered on in Wales and some
other districts. Queen Bertha of Kent had been baptized as a
child in France and by the terms of her marriage settlement was
allowed to practise her religion and to keep Bishop Liudhard at
her court as chaplain and instructor. King Ethelbert, therefore,
though himself a pagan, was familiar with the idea of Christianity,
and he consented to receive St. Augustine, not in his capital city,
but in the Isle of Thanet, then separated from the mainland by a
channel nearly a mile wide. The meeting was held in the open
air to avert the dangers of witchcraft; tradition says that the King
sat under an ancient oak, while opposite to him stood Augustine
and his monks, bearing a large silver cross and a gilded picture of
Our Lord. In this place the second conversion of our land was
begun. Ethelbert heard Augustine's words translated to him by

the interpreters and then, without committing himself further, gave permission for the monks to come to Canterbury and preach to any who would hear them. In due course he was himself converted, and with him the majority of his people. The King was baptized on Whit-Sunday, June 2nd, A.D. 597, and St. Gregory records that on the following Christmas Day ten thousand of his subjects were christened in the waters of the River Swale.

The conversion of other parts of England followed much the same pattern. The King permitted or invited the missionaries to enter his land, and being himself convinced, was followed to the font by most of his people. King Edwin was the mainspring of the conversion in Northumbria, as King Saeberht was in Essex and King Peada in Mercia. Men followed their lord into religion as into battle; it was scarcely thinkable at that period that they should be of one faith and he of another. That such wholesale conversions were not always very deep is obvious. Men worshipped Christ sincerely enough in prosperity, but often reverted secretly to more ancient rites in times of trouble. Bede tells us that Redwald of East Anglia tried to make the best of both worlds, for "in one temple he had erected an altar for the sacrifices of Christ and another little altar for burnt sacrifices to his idols and devils."[1] What a king could do openly, lesser men probably did in private, and the reiterated fulminations of princes and bishops throughout the following four or five centuries show how firm was the hold of the older gods and how difficult they were to defeat. Moreover, the kings' strong influence worked both ways, and if a ruler apostatized, or was succeeded by a pagan son, the light of Christianity failed or burnt but dimly in that kingdom during his reign, while a successful invasion from outside was often quite as much a religious as a political upheaval.

It was this element of continual struggle, alike in men's souls and on the battle-field, that made the early saints so much more than mere examples to the devout. They were the heroes of the faith, whose fiery words and burning zeal inspired their followers and kept the light of religion burning in times that were often very dark indeed. This was especially true of the native saints and

[1] *Ecclesiastical History.*

martyrs, or those who brought the Gospel to our shores. Such men were of necessity strong-minded and virile as well as holy, and it was their heroic qualities of courage, generosity, wisdom and strength that were chiefly remembered after they were dead. During their lives they were leaders of thought and sometimes leaders in battle; after their deaths their graves became shrines at which miracles were wrought and the sick, the halt and the blind were cured of their ills. They took the place of the older heroes of paganism and not infrequently inherited their legends; sometimes they superseded the ancient gods as patrons of wells and other holy places. They appeared in visions to the doubtful or the unhappy; occasionally they struck down their traducers from beyond the tomb, as St. Edmund did with King Sweyn. Their remembered words were twisted to form the basis of successful prophecies. Perfectly genuine incidents of their earthly careers were embroidered and coloured with miraculous hues, or were overlaid with myths borrowed from that very paganism against which they had striven and fought. In short, they became folk-heroes along with Arthur and the rest of that varied company, and as such they commanded the warm and unquestioning admiration of those who followed, at however great a distance, along the trail which they had blazed.

Such a hero-saint was King Oswald of Northumbria. St. Paulinus had converted his people in the reign of Edwin, but they had fallen away in the years following Edwin's death. Oswald reclaimed them by his example and the fervent ardour of his own belief. At the beginning of his reign, before the Battle of Denisesburn, St. Columba appeared to him in a vision and promised him victory, and the Witan, to whom he hastened with the story, agreed to be baptized with all the people if the promise was fulfilled. Oswald's own personal followers seem to have been Christians, for Bede tells us that he had "an army, small indeed, but fenced with the faith of Christ."[1] On the morning of the battle the King gathered these men round him and set up a hastily made cross, holding it firm with his own hands while the soldiers beat down the earth round its foot. Then they all prayed together, and later in the day the much larger army of Caedwalla was signally

[1] *Ecclesiastical History.*

defeated. The cross was left standing, and through it many miracles were afterwards performed. Bede says that in his own day men took away chips of its wood, or the moss which grew on it, and used them to cure diseases of various kinds. The field itself was known as Heavenfield, and was regarded with great reverence by all Northumbrians.

After his victory Oswald set to work to convert his people, and summoned St. Aidan from Iona to teach them. There is a delightful story in Bede's *History* to the effect that at first a "man of more austere stomach" was sent. His mission was not a success. Evidently he did not know how to manage the hardy northerners, for he could make no headway with them; they refused to listen to his preaching, and he retaliated by calling them "folks that might not be reclaimed, of a hard capacity and fierce nature." He returned, therefore, to his own country, perhaps to study the uses of tact and understanding, and was replaced by St. Aidan, a man "chiefly garnished with the grace of discretion, the mother of all virtues."

Under Oswald, Northumbria became a strong and united country and the chief champion of Christianity in England. He extended its boundaries, reconciled its quarrelling inhabitants and, by force of arms and by wise government, made it a power not lightly to be attacked by other monarchs. His prosperous reign came to an end on August 5th, A.D. 642, when he fell fighting against Penda, the pagan King of Mercia at the Battle of Maserfield. The exact location of this battle has never been certainly decided; Shropshire claims it for Oswestry, and Lancashire for Winwick, near Warrington. In both places there is a well dedicated to St. Oswald near a church of the same name. That at Winwick is in a field on Hermitage Farm, about half a mile from the church. In former times it was a well-known healing well, and its water is still sometimes used locally as a cure for sore eyes. The well at Oswestry was covered, in Leland's time, by a chapel, and the ruins of this building were still to be seen in the late eighteenth century. The spring itself was almost certainly a pagan holy place renamed for the saint, for divination was practised there, and it was a wishing as well as a healing well. A hundred years ago the feeble and infirm and those with failing sight came regularly to bathe in it, and bottles of its water were sent away to those who could not come in person.

As a wishing well it still retains some attraction, though some of the clearly magical ceremonies connected with it are now nearly forgotten. One method of obtaining a wish used in the late nineteenth century was to state the desire in a whisper through a small hole in the keystone of the arch that spanned the water. Another way was to bathe the face whilst wishing, or to throw a stone on a certain green spot, thus causing a jet of water to spring up, under which the devotee had to put his head. At the back of the well is a stone from which a carved head wearing a crown once projected. Tradition says that at this spot King Oswald's head was buried. A sure way of obtaining a wish was to go at midnight to the spring and, taking up some water in the hand, drink a little and throw the rest against the stone. If all the water fell on the place where the carved head formerly was without touching any other part of the well the wish would infallibly be granted. To know whether or not the fulfilment of a desire might be relied upon, the inquirer could search for an empty beech-husk which resembled a human face, and float it upon the water with the face uppermost. He then counted up to twenty; if the husk was still floating at the end his wish would be granted, but if it had already sunk, there was no hope of it.

These customs savour of magic, and it is clear that the Christian saint has here inherited the functions of an ancient pagan water-spirit. Brand mentions another well dedicated to St. Oswald at Rosebery Topping, in Yorkshire, where a sick man's shirt used to be thrown into the water to see whether its owner would recover or die. If it floated all would be well; if it sank, the patient was doomed. The legends of St. Oswald's healing powers seem to have sprung up very quickly after his death, for Bede tells us that many miracles were wrought at the place where he died. In his *History* he mentions the healing well at Maserfield, though unfortunately he gives us no clue as to where this battle-field was. He tells us that "many took up the very dust of the place where his body fell, and putting it into water, did much good with it to their friends who were sick." So persistent was this custom of carrying away the sacred earth that by degrees a hole was made "as deep as the height of a man." Men and beasts alike were cured there, and Bede adds that it was no wonder they received this grace from the dead king, "for, whilst he lived, he never ceased to provide for the poor and infirm, and to bestow alms on them and assist them."

The King's great charity is commemorated in another legend, that of St. Oswald's Hand. On one occasion, when he was sitting at meat with St. Aidan on Easter Sunday, he heard that a number of poor people were waiting outside. He immediately ordered the food from his own table to be distributed to them, and the silver dish in which it was served to be cut up and divided amongst them. St. Aidan thereupon blessed the hand that gave so freely, saying "May this hand never perish." Nor did it, for after his death Oswald's right arm was preserved, uncorrupted, in St. Peter's Church at Bamborough. In our own time the legend is commemorated at Lower Peover Church in Cheshire by a wooden hand nailed to the wall, which is supposed to represent St. Oswald's miraculous hand. In actual fact, it is probably one of those wooden hands which, in the Middle Ages, were set up at fairs to denote that all might enter freely to trade, without molestation from the local Guild Merchant, for so long as the fair lasted. A hand made of rushes is one of the traditional "rushbearings" still carried at Grasmere during the Rushbearing procession held annually on the Saturday nearest St. Oswald's Day, August 5th.

Two hundred and twenty-eight years after the Northumbrian king's death, another English king suffered martyrdom for his religion during the bitter struggles against the invading Danes. St. Edmund, King of East Anglia, was crowned on Christmas Day, A.D. 856, when he was fifteen years old. Fourteen years later the Danish army under Hingwar and Hubba marched through his kingdom and took up their winter quarters at Thetford. Northumbria had already fallen, Mercia had made a temporary treaty with the invaders, the armies of Wessex were far away. There was no help anywhere for the East Anglian king, and we have no record that he ever asked for any. Unaided, he struck at the Danish camp and was defeated and captured. He was offered his freedom if he would consent to rule under the victors, or to deny his faith, and having proudly refused to do either, he was shot to death with arrows. His body was then beheaded and contemptuously thrown into a thicket. The surrounding country was ravaged by the triumphant Danes: churches, homes and monasteries were sacked, the great Abbey of Medehamsted plundered and burnt. East Anglia lay under the heel of the pagan, and henceforward the entire hope of England was centred in the young and comparatively unknown Prince of Wessex, afterwards called Alfred the Great.

King Edmund's death made a great impression on his contemporaries, and he was universally acclaimed a martyr for his faith. There is no doubt that the fall of East Anglia was simply an incident in the general Danish invasion, but later legends have tried to find a more personal reason for it. Roger of Wendover[1] tells us that it sprang in the first instance from the treachery of one of Edmund's own men. According to his account, the Danish king, Lodbrog, was swept by a sudden storm on to the shores of Norfolk and was hospitably received by the East Anglian king. One day, when out hunting with Bern, Edmund's chief huntsman, Lodbrog was murdered by the latter, who was jealous of his superior skill in the hunting field. The crime was discovered through the devotion of the dead man's dog, which refused to leave his body, and Bern was condemned to be put into Lodbrog's boat, without sail or oar, to live or die as God willed. The chances of wind and weather took the murderer to Denmark, and there he had his revenge. He told Hingwar and Hubba, Lodbrog's sons, that their father had been killed by Edmund's orders, and offered to act as guide to any punitive expedition they chose to send. Contrary winds drove the avenging fleet to Northumbria, where the Danes stayed to ravage and plunder, but never for a moment did they lose sight of their original objective. In the following year they invaded East Anglia. After much bitter fighting, Hingwar offered Edmund a share of his treasure if he would submit and be his vassal. The English king refused, and, being later captured, was tortured and finally killed by his implacable enemies.

Tradition says that his body, with the head severed from the trunk, was thrown into the thickest part of the woods at Eglesdene. When the Danes had departed the East Anglians set out to look

[1] Roger of Wendover, *Flores Historiarum*.

for their martyred lord, and eventually found his body in the woods. The head they could not find until a strange voice was heard crying, "Here, here, here" from the depths of a thorn-thicket. Thither they went, and saw the head, guarded by a wolf which made no effort to attack them, but suffered them to take it away, following the mournful procession back to Hoxne and leaving only when the relic had been reverently deposited with the body. A little while later head and body were found to be miraculously reunited, a thin purple line, like a thread, showing where the original severance had been.

In A.D. 903 the martyred king's body was removed to Beodrics-worth, now known to us as Bury St. Edmunds, and housed in a wooden shrine which quickly became a place of pilgrimage. Later on, a stone church was built for it, and this was replaced by another of greater magnificence in the time of Baldwin, the first Norman Abbot. In 1222 the Council of Oxford declared November 20th the anniversary of the saint's death, to be one of the holy days of precept throughout England, and the feast was annually observed at Bury St. Edmunds with great religious fervour and popular revels of a somewhat less hallowed character. Jocelyn de Brakelonde tells us that in the twelfth century Abbot Sampson caused the tomb to be opened at midnight in the presence of a number of monks. The body was found to be quite uncorrupted, the head united to it, and the feet pointing stiffly upwards, like those of a man newly dead. Such incorruptibility was considered in the Middle Ages to be a sure sign of sainthood, as were also the numerous miracles performed at the shrine, or by means of relics.

The folk-lore traditions of St. Edmund are somewhat curious. Of his personal character we know nothing, except that he was obviously a man of great courage and determination. But it may be significant that two of the best known of his legends, apart from his miraculous cures, are concerned with the punishment of offenders. In the reign of Aethelstan, Leofstan, Sheriff of Suffolk, was struck with instant madness for attempting to seize an accused woman who had fled for sanctuary to the saint's shrine. In 1014 King Sweyn died suddenly at Gainsborough, probably of a stroke. The men of his family seem to have been liable to such seizures, and it may well be that something of the kind overtook the Danish king in the moment of his greatest triumph. Tradition, however, says that it was St. Edmund who killed him. Shortly before his death he had exacted heavy tribute from Bury St. Edmunds, and had not only threatened to burn the town and the shrine if it was not paid, but had declared that St. Edmund was not a saint at all. What happened thereafter is best told in the words of Roger de Hoveden. In his *Annals* he says:

> At length towards the evening of the day on which, in a general council he held at a place called Geagnesbury he had again repeated these threats, while surrounded with most numerous crowds of Danes, he alone beheld Saint Edmund coming armed towards him; on seeing whom he was terrified, and began to cry out with loud shrieks, exclaiming "Fellow-soldiers, to the rescue, to the rescue! Behold St. Edmund has come to slay me"; after saying which, being pierced by the Saint with a spear, he fell from the throne upon which he was sitting, and suffering great torments until nightfall, on the third day before the nones of February, terminated his life by a shocking death.

In local popular belief the warrior-king seems to have been associated, rather oddly, with marriage and fertility. Saints and heroes often inherited pagan traditions, as we have seen, but usually the connecting link was slightly more obvious than it was in this case. Possibly the fact that St. Edmund was a king as well as a saint may have had something to do with it, for in primitive communities kings were supposed, by their strength and virtue,. or lack of them, to affect the fertility of men and crops. A superstition still prevalent at the end of last century prevented any bride and bridegroom from crossing Gold Bridge, in Hoxne parish, on their way to or from their wedding. To do so entailed certain misfortune. Legend said that St. Edmund had hidden under one of the arches of this bridge after the defeat at Thetford, and had been betrayed by a newly married couple who saw his gilded spurs gleaming in the moonlight. As a punishment for their treachery he laid a curse upon every bride and groom who should in future cross the bridge on their wedding day. The exact nature of the promised evil was not stated, but in similar legends elsewhere the most usual form is the early death of one of the partners, the barrenness of the wife, or the birth of imbecile children. Whether

St. Edmund here replaced some ancient and inimical water-spirit, or whether the whole story sprang from a dim memory of foundation sacrifice is uncertain. Whatever the legend's origin, it seems to have played upon the fears of the local people for more than a thousand years, and possibly still does so, for, even in this sceptical age, few things are so tough as superstitions which concern courtship, marriage and childbirth.

The peculiar custom known as the Oblation of the White Bull savours even more strongly of paganism. That it persisted in Bury St. Edmunds till the very eve of the Reformation is shown by three indentures concerning the manor of Haberden in the Registers of the monastery. One of these was drawn up in the early years of Henry VII's reign, the other two in that of Henry VIII. All three refer to the tenant's obligation to "find or cause to be found one white bull every year of his term, so often as it shall happen that any gentlewoman, or any other woman, from devotion or vows by them made, shall visit the tomb of the glorious martyr St. Edmund, to make oblation of the said white bull."[1] This bull was not to be used for the ordinary work of the farm or for bull-baiting, but was to enjoy full ease and plenty in the fields until it was needed. When a married woman desired a child it was adorned with garlands and ribbons and led in procession through the streets to the principal gate of the monastery. Before it went the monks, singing; the woman herself walked beside it, stroking its sides and dewlaps, and a great crowd of citizens followed after. At the monastery gate the bull was turned back, while the supplicant went into the church and made her vows before St. Edmund's shrine, kissing the stones and praying for the blessing of a child. Here clearly we have an ancient fertility rite grafted upon the cult of a popular local saint, in much the same way as a kindred rite at Coventry had been grafted upon the legend of a local great lady. The somewhat loose character of the revels on November 20th may also have some connexion with the dead king's association with fertility, an association the more curious in that the whole of St. Edmund's recorded history is concerned only with warfare and religion.

---

[1] Reverend W. Hawkins, *Corolla Varia*, 1634. Extracts translated and printed in *The Gentleman's Magazine*, November 1783.

Singularly few folk-tales are told of Alfred the Great. Even the celebrated story of the cakes comes to us not from folk-tradition but from the so-called *Annals of St. Neots*, written in the early twelfth century, which Archbishop Parker mistakenly believed to be the work of Bishop Asser, Alfred's friend and biographer. Yet of all the Saxon kings, this truly great man might have been expected to develop into a folk-hero of the conventional type, with all the tales of divine or fairy birth and magical attributes which ordinarily belong to that status. He was the centre of England's resistance in the darkest days of the Danish invasion. At one period, so reduced that he was forced to hide in woods and marshes with his house-thegns, he lived to see his country restored through his efforts to independence and peace. It was at the time when his fortunes were at their lowest ebb that he was heartened by a vision of Our Lady who appeared to him at Athelney. Legend says that he flung his last remaining jewel at her feet, and centuries later a gold and enamel locket believed to be his was found in the marshes. It was probably at this time also that he came to Stourton, in Wiltshire, and, being thirsty, prayed for water, whereupon the springs now known as Six Wells sprang up to refresh him. The power of calling water into being is one of the well-known attributes of saints and folk-heroes, and many wells in this and other countries traditionally owe their existence to the fact that some such individual rested on the spot, or simply struck the ground with his staff.

Alfred was no less great as a ruler than as a fighter. Himself unlettered, he loved learning and founded many schools. He diligently sought out scholars from Ireland, Wales and the Continent, and brought them to England to restore the old, lost knowledge of the people. He learnt to read at the age of thirty-nine, and thereafter translated the Histories of Bede and Orosius, collected many of the older national epics, and began, or caused to be begun, the *Anglo-Saxon Chronicle*. He reformed the army of his day and founded a fleet. He codified and amended the laws and was, as Asser tells us, "as wise in following up judicial matters as in all other things."[1] In a country full of jarring elements he was trusted by all men, the poor no less than the rich, perhaps

[1] Bishop Asser, *Life of Alfred.*

148

because they realized that he was not only fundamentally just, but also intensely interested in them and their concerns. It was this quality of abiding interest in everything that went on round him, an interest that triumphed constantly over his physical delicacy and attacks of pain, which was one of Alfred's most striking attributes. His deep religious feeling expressed itself not only in the building of many churches and monasteries, but also in his own way of life. Asser tells us that "in so far as his sickness and his means would allow, he promised to render with all his might to God the half part of his services, whether of mind or body, by day or by night", and in order to keep this vow he had candles constantly burning in lanterns made of white ox-horn for the proper division of the hours. Yet he was no fanatical ascetic; he loved hunting and cheerful company and spent much time on mechanical inventions of his own, or working in gold. Strangers from all parts came to his court and were entertained; he listened eagerly to their tales of foreign places and adventure, as he did to those of the explorers and merchants whom he encouraged and inspired. He died peacefully in A.D. 901, leaving behind him a country better than he found it and a name that has endured untarnished for a thousand years. In spite of wars, sickness and the myriad difficulties of kingship in those times, his must have been a happy life, for he was never bored and he accomplished most, if not all, the tasks he had set himself. Of him, perhaps more than of most men, it might truly be said "He was a good man and did good things."

Two English kings besides St. Edmund bear the proud title of martyr, though they died at the hands of their own countrymen; another was proclaimed a saint by his people, though not by Rome. King Charles I, who died for his principles, both religious and political, came too far down in history to have miracles ascribed to him after death. He lives in folk-tradition mainly in ghost stories and tales of omens fulfilled, and in the belief current in the time of the Commonwealth that handkerchiefs soaked in his blood by the devout at his execution cured many and diverse diseases. Edward the Martyr was in a different position. He was the son of Edgar the Peaceful and Eneda, his handfast wife, and he had the misfortune to be caught up in the remains of the bitter controversy between monk and canon that had raged in his father's time. The Witan chose him for their king rather than Ethelred, his young stepbrother, a decision naturally distasteful to his stepmother, Elfryth, who had hoped her own child would reign. Tradition says she murdered him, but of this there is no definite proof. She may have been suspected at the time, but she was not openly accused. The first person to connect her with the murder, and then only by implication, was Osbern, the biographer of St. Dunstan, who wrote more than eighty years after the event, when William I was on the throne. Edward was the choice of one party in the state, and there were plenty of people in the other party who had as much to gain by his death as Elfryth. He seems to have been genuinely fond of her and to have trusted her, and certainly there was a very real affection between him and the child Ethelred.

Whoever was the prime mover in the affair, he was murdered at Corfe Gate on March 18th, A.D. 978. He had been hunting with Wulfstan, his jester, and had sent the latter to find food. Wulfstan did not return, and, becoming weary of waiting, the young king rode on to Corfe Gate alone. It was then evening. He would not stay at the house because it was late, but still mounted on his horse, he drank a cup of wine outside. While he was doing so he was stabbed by one of the men who had come out to meet him. His horse, startled by his sudden fall from the saddle, bolted down the steep hill, dragging the body with one foot caught in the stirrup behind it. It is still said in Dorset that a ghostly horse can be heard on occasion galloping down the hill from Corfe Castle. The terrified animal was eventually stopped by some countrymen who did not recognize the battered and bloody face of their king, but realized from his clothing that here was a man of rank. They were afraid to be mixed up in so dangerous an affair, and when they heard riders approaching from Corfe Gate they left the body where it was on the road and fled.

What was happening meanwhile at the house we do not know, but we can guess. Tradition says that Ethelred cried for his dead brother and was so unmercifully beaten by his mother with a heavy candle that he had a horror of candles throughout his life and would never have them near him. The men whom the peasants saw must have been sent out by Elfryth to investigate, and we can only assume, from later evidence, that they hastily buried the body at the roadside, without ceremony and without anything to mark the spot. The King of England had simply disappeared, killed, it was given out, by a fall from his horse. Wild rumours ran through the country, but nothing could be proved. Ethelred was accepted as king; his coronation was fixed for the fourteenth of April at Kingston-on-Thames. St. Dunstan crowned him, but there was no true blessing in that hallowing. The aged saint prophesied evil for the new king because, he said, he had climbed to the throne through the death of his brother and his mother's plots. All the days of his life the sword should never lie in the scabbard, a prophecy only too well fulfilled in the harassed reign of Ethelred the Unready. That evening a fiery cloud was seen in the sky, shaped like a bloody hand, a dreadful omen at any time and doubly so after St. Dunstan's awful words.

Some months later rumours of miraculous cures at a spot on the Wareham road began to spread through the country. There was nothing to be seen there except reeds, yet the afflicted went there in faith and came back whole. Elfryth heard these tales and determined to see for herself whether what she must have suspected was true. But her horse refused to move under her, and when she called for another, the second animal did the same. The rumours reached the ears of St. Dunstan, who sent men to dig at the spot. Guided by the slanting rays of the sun they found the body of a young man whom those who had known him in life recognized as the dead king. His body was quite uncorrupted, like those of the saints; a dagger wound in the stomach bore mute evidence to the fact that more than a fall from his horse had caused his death That he had been murdered was clear, but no man knew who had murdered him; he could not be avenged by his own people, and it was left to the Danes to be his unconscious avengers in the troubled years that followed. In virtue of his violent death, his uncorrupted body and the miracles at his grave, he was everywhere regarded as a saint. "He was in life an earthly king;" says the *Anglo-Saxon Chronicle*, "he is now after death a heavenly saint. Him would not his earthly kinsmen avenge, but him hath his heavenly Father greatly avenged." In fact, he seems to have been a cheerful and pleasant young man, who was murdered for purely political reasons, to the great detriment of his country which lost a far better king in him than it gained in Ethelred the Unready. But to the people of his own time he was a martyr, and as Edward the Martyr he is still known to us to-day.

Five centuries later another king was "canonized" by his people, and might have been so officially had the Commission of Enquiry appointed to investigate the claims made on his behalf begun their work a little earlier. In 1471 the gentle and scholarly Henry VI was murdered, as all men believed, by Richard, Duke of Gloucester. On the very day on which Edward IV rode in triumph into London after his victory at Barnet, the last of the Lancastrian kings died very conveniently, by violence, according to his friends, "of pure displeasure and melancholy," according to his Yorkist enemies, who were also his jailers at the time. When his body lay in state in St. Paul's Cathedral it bled in the sight of the people, a sure sign for those who saw it that he had been foully murdered. Thereafter he was hastily buried at Chertsey, and within a very short time tales of miracles performed at his grave began to circulate. So persistent were these stories that in 1474 the body was exhumed by the Duke of Gloucester who, by doing so, merely confirmed the popular belief that the dead king was a saint, for the body is said to have been largely incorrupt and exhaling a sweet odour. It was transferred to Windsor, and there also there were miracles which attracted an ever-increasing number of pilgrims.

Paintings and statues of the unhappy king appeared in many churches, and lights were kept burning before them. The dagger with which he was killed was preserved as a sacred relic in the Augustinian Chapel on Caversham Bridge. Prayers that he had composed were commonly used, and hymns were sung to or about him. In 1479 the Archbishop of York found it necessary to issue an order forbidding the veneration of "the image of Henry, lately King of England in fact, but not by right", but this, like other similar admonitions, was quite useless. The people continued to make pilgrimages to Windsor, to "bend a coin" to the murdered king and to invoke him in times of trouble or of danger.

Though Henry VI was never canonized, there was much in his character that was of the true stuff of which saints are made. Like

Henry VI: Hero of Charity and Healing

153

Alfred the Great, he loved learning and religion, and his abiding memorials to-day are King's College, Cambridge, and Eton College, both of which he founded. He was deeply pious, amiable, kindly and generous to a fault. He cared much for the welfare of children and of weak and helpless people; he hated all forms of violence, and the idea of warfare between Christians was intolerable to him. He never bore malice, and genuinely forgave those—and they were many—who injured him. Had he been born a private citizen he would have been perfectly happy as a scholar or a monk. It was his misfortune that he was set on the throne of England before he was a year old and forced to rule in an age when only a strong man could have hoped to succeed. As a king he was a failure. He lacked firmness and was too easily swayed by those whose characters were stronger than his own. Moreover, he was subject to recurring fits of apathetic melancholy, a taint inherited from his grandfather, Charles VI of France, and while these lasted he was incapable of dealing adequately either with his own or with State affairs. But all such failings were forgotten in the pity excited by his unhappy last days and his tragic death, and what endured in men's memories were his very real virtues, which stood out the more sharply against the brutalities of his time.

Such spontaneous veneration of his defeated rival was naturally distasteful to Edward IV, but in Henry VII's time the royal policy was altered. Henry Tudor was quite willing to believe his uncle was a saint, since no political harm could come to him through doing so. He approached the Pope on the subject of canonization, and in 1494 a Commission of Enquiry was set up by Alexander VI, and sanctioned again in 1504 by Julius II. Witnesses were carefully examined concerning the reported miracles, and the result of these examinations still exists in the long list of miracles contained in the HarleianMSS.[1] Men described to the Commissioners how they or their beasts had been cured of various diseases after invoking the dead king, how they had been delivered from prison or shipwreck, freed from possession by evil spirits, or had lost and stolen property restored to them. Some had seen their children or their friends raised from the dead, or lunatics made sane; others had been saved from drowning or the effect of wounds. William

[1] *De Miraculis Beatissimi Militis Xpi Henrici Vj*. Harleian MSS.

Edwards, Vicar of Hollington, had sight and speech restored to him after his eyes had been blinded and his tongue cut out by three men who attacked him on All Saints Day, 1488. All the miracles recorded in the existing list occurred between 1481 and 1500; if there were any later ones we do not know of them.

Henry VII's Chapel at Westminster was originally intended to house his uncle's remains, but the body was never actually brought there. The process of canonization was slow and expensive, and whether for this reason, or because men's minds were already turning towards the coming religious changes, it was finally abandoned in 1528. Gradually pilgrims ceased to visit the tomb at Windsor or to invoke King Henry in their difficulties. The Reformation, which swept away the far stronger cult of Simon de Montfort, whose miraculous tomb and healing well at Evesham were visited for three centuries by the afflicted, withered that of Henry VI while it was still young. In less than a hundred years after his death it had not only ceased completely but was already nearly forgotten.

CHAPTER X

ST. THOMAS OF CANTERBURY

ONE of the most interesting of the English saint-hero cults was that of St. Thomas of Canterbury. It sprang into being on a single night of violence and murder, and lasted for more than three hundred years. It made Canterbury famous throughout Europe during the later Middle Ages and attracted innumerable pilgrims to its central shrine, not only from our own country but from many others as well. Up to the time of the Reformation, St. Thomas's popularity in England was second only to that of St. George. Yet in life he had not been by any means universally beloved, nor was the cause for which he died one which the people at large had very much at heart. He was by nature hot-tempered, proud and aggressive, and he seems to have been singularly lacking in the gentler virtues usually associated with saints. He was a fierce hater and a savage upholder of his own and the Church's rights, and in defence of these he was prepared to go to almost any lengths. He was temperamentally incapable of seeing more than one side of any question in which he took real interest, and his tenacity of purpose, no less than his occasionally hasty judgments, sometimes betrayed him into acts of peculiar injustice. Nevertheless, after his death, the ordinary people unanimously proclaimed him a saint and a martyr, and the official canonization, when it came, did little more than endorse an already firmly-held popular belief. Courage he certainly had in full measure and complete devotion to his own ideals, and these qualities, combined with the horror of his murder, were enough to make him a hero to the men of his own and the three succeeding centuries.

Thomas à Becket was a man of very great ability, who for eight years was Henry II's Chancellor. During the whole of that not inconsiderable period he was a devoted and true friend to the King and a faithful servant of his country. His life at that time was not unduly austere and he lived more like a wealthy layman of high position than a cleric. There is no evidence that he then aspired to special holiness, or was anything more than a capable and ambitious statesman; if a few discerning people suspected that he had it in him to win a martyr's crown they can have had little reason for supposing that he would ever actually do so. But when in 1162 he was made Archbishop of Canterbury, something resembling a conversion seems to have occurred. His whole way of life was radically altered, and with it his political outlook. He became extremely devout and practised rigorous austerities, wearing a hair-shirt under his clothes, fasting and doing penance, and endearing himself to the poor by lavish almsgiving. The devotion he had previously given to the King was now given entirely to the Church. He regarded himself as its champion, and more particularly as the protector of every privilege of the See of Canterbury. His sole ambition was to see the Church made independent of all State control, and for this single purpose he was prepared to make whatever drastic sacrifices of himself and others that might prove to be necessary.

Of his long and bitter quarrel with the King it is not necessary to speak at length. Given the characters of the two men and their divergent aims, it was inevitable that there should be dissentions, and, in fact, these began almost as soon as Becket was made Archbishop. They flared into an open breach in 1164 over the question of the immunity of the clergy from secular punishment. Becket desired to see the clergy entirely free from the jurisdiction of ordinary law courts and to make it impossible for them to be tried for any crime, however heinous, except in ecclesiastical courts, which had no power to inflict heavier penalties than excommunication or deprivation of orders. This idea was not new, but in the Archbishop's hands it took an extreme form, and in practice would have meant that a very large number of the King's subjects were outside his laws, since not only ordained priests and monks, but also deacons and minor church officials were thus made immune from the punishments suffered by laymen. In 1164 the Great Council met at Clarendon and drew up a document which was in effect a compromise between Becket's demands and the natural wishes of the King. It proposed that clerics accused of secular crimes should first be tried in ecclesiastical courts, where their guilt or innocence could be established, and that if they were proved guilty they should then be handed over to the King's officers for punishment. Where laymen and clerics were involved in lawsuits the matter was to be judged in secular courts, and the consent of the King was to be obtained before barons could be excommunicated or punished for purely spiritual offences.

Such, in outline, were the famous Constitutions of Clarendon, which now seem to us eminently reasonable, having regard to the circumstances and opinions of the time. Becket signed them, but the next day he withdrew his consent, saying he had committed a deadly sin in agreeing to them in the first place. At the Northampton Council in the following October he defied the King and then fled to France, where he remained for six years, doing his best to stir up the French King and the Pope against his own sovereign. In 1170 a shaky reconciliation was effected, and he returned to Canterbury.

All this had little to do with the ordinary people, who would not have benefited in any way had St. Thomas's desires been fulfilled. Their opinions on the quarrel were probably rather vague, though it is doubtful whether, even at that period, the average layman really wished to see the clergy in a position so vastly superior to his own. But these were high matters on which his views were never directly sought by those most intimately concerned, and he could be little more than a spectator of the battle raging between the two greatest powers in the land. A few, indeed, were themselves involved, for Becket, in the course of his struggles for the greater power of Canterbury, laid claim to a number of estates on the ground that they were, or had formerly been, Church lands, and not only went to law with their owners, but freely used the more dreadful weapon of excommunication against all who dared to oppose him. Like Henry, he was a man of violent and headstrong temperament, and he allowed no considerations of friendship or policy to deflect him by one hair's-breadth from his chosen path. Fitzstephen relates how, only a few hours before his death, John of Salisbury, one of his most faithful followers reproached him because he would never take any man's advice, but always did what seemed good to himself alone.

Nevertheless, if he had many enemies he also had many admirers. His austerities, his almsgiving, and his single-hearted devotion to the cause he had made his own appealed to the popular imagination. Both sides passionately believed themselves to be in the right, and if modern opinion naturally agrees with the King rather than with the saint, there can have been no such unanimity of thought in the twelfth century. When Becket arrived in Canterbury after his voluntary exile, he was received with the greatest enthusiasm by the townspeople. On his way to the palace he rode through streets gay with banners and noisy with the sound of bells and trumpets, and all along the road resounded the welcoming cheers of the citizens who were genuinely glad to see their Archbishop back again after six long years.

But if they, or their King, imagined that an era of peace was thus inaugurated they were soon undeceived. In the previous June, Henry had arranged that his eldest son should be crowned and reign with him as his colleague. The right of crowning England's kings lay with the See of Canterbury, but in Becket's absence the ceremony was performed by the Archbishop of York and the Bishops of London and Salisbury. In a furious rage at what he considered a deliberate infringement of his privileges, Becket induced the Pope to excommunicate the three prelates, and the letters authorizing this were actually in his possession at the time of his reconciliation with Henry. His first care on arriving in England was to arrange for their delivery to the astonished and indignant bishops, who were then in Dover and who were naturally not slow in informing the King of this fresh declaration of war.

This unhappy beginning was followed by more trouble. News reached the Archbishop that a ship bearing a present of wine from Henry to himself had been seized by Randulf de Broc, one of his most hated enemies, and her crew imprisoned at Saltwood Castle. This injury was promptly righted by the young King, but fresh fuel was added to the fire by another member of the de Broc family, who, on Christmas Eve, either from a desire to insult Becket openly or as a peculiarly ill-timed jest, cut off the tails of a horse and a sumpter-mule from his stables.

This was a cruel and stupid outrage particularly likely to wound the Archbishop who loved horses, and it seems to have made a deep impression on his mind. The next day, being Christmas Day, he preached a bitter and violent sermon to the large congregation assembled for the Christmas services. He spoke of his saintly predecessors in the cathedral and made the curious statement that Canterbury already had one martyr (St. Alphege) and might soon have another. Then he related the story of the docked animals and pronounced sentence of excommunication upon Robert and Randulf de Broc, as well as on two priests who had rashly accepted parishes without his authority. Finally he denounced the three bishops and solemnly cursed in Christ's name all those who sowed discord between the King and himself, saying that their names should be blotted from the assembly of the saints, and flinging the candle before him to the ground as a symbol of their total extinction. Then he descended from the pulpit, and as he made his way to the altar he repeated his strange remark about another martyr to Alexander, his cross-bearer. The congregation was thrown into a state of great alarm by this extraordinary sermon, with its dark hints and bitter accusations, coming as it did so unexpectedly in the season of goodwill and so soon after the Archbishop's apparently peaceful return to his city. Many wept, and others showed that that they had guessed at the personal application of his prophecy by asking why he thought of deserting them, and to whose care he would leave them when he was gone. Four days later they were to be reminded of his words and to see the prophecy most dreadfully and exactly fulfilled.

Tradition has it that de Broc's insult was not the only one of its kind that had been offered to the Archbishop. The people of Strood were said to have cut off the tail of his horse when he rode through their town, and to have borne children with horses' tails in consequence. Polydore Vergil tells us that:

> There were some to whom it seemed that the king's secret wish was that Thomas should be got rid of. He, indeed, as one accounted to be an enemy of the king's person, was already regarded with so little respect, nay, was treated with so much contempt that when he came to Strood, which village is situated on the Medway, the river that washes Rochester, the inhabitants of the place, being eager to show some mark of contumely to the prelate in his disgrace, did not scruple to cut off the tail of the horse on which he was riding; but by this profane and inhospitable act they covered themselves with eternal reproach, for it so happened after this, by the will of God, that all the offspring born from the men who had done this thing were born with tails like brute animals. But this mark of infamy, which formerly was everywhere notorious, has disappeared with the extinction of the race whose fathers perpetrated the deed.[1]

This story is obviously borrowed from other sources, for it is also told of St. Augustine, with the slight variation that the men of Strood threw fish-tails at him, and their children were afterwards tailed like fishes. Another version says it was the people of Dorset who were so afflicted for a similar offence against the missionary-saint. Devonshire children were once taught that all Cornishmen had tails, though the reason for this unfortunate distinction does not seem to have been preserved. Legends of tailed men occur in other countries also and seem to be connected with the ancient belief in werewolves. To suspect a man of having a tail evidently persisted as a ready form of insult up to a comparatively late period, for in the sixteenth century John Bale, the reforming Bishop of Ossory, complained bitterly, in his *Actes of English Votaries*, that as a result of former monkish fabrications decent Englishmen could not travel anywhere abroad without having it thrown in their faces that all their race were tailed.

At this Christmas season of 1170, Henry II was at Bur, near Bayeux, and there the three excommunicated bishops found him.

---

[1] *Anglicae Historiae*, 1534.

As soon as he heard their news he flew into one of those appalling rages from which all the men of his line suffered on occasion and which were supposed to spring from the demon blood that ran in their veins. It was then that he uttered the fatal sentence accusing his followers of cowardice because none of them would deliver him from "this low-born priest". That he intended anyone to act upon these words is very improbable, and, indeed, the demoniac character of his rages makes it unlikely that he had any clear realization of what he said while they lasted. But the words were spoken and could not be recalled, and that night four knights—William de Tracy, Reginald Fitzurse, Hugh de Moreville and Richard le Bret—slipped away from the castle and crossed to England. They went first to Saltwood, the home of the excommunicated de Brocs, and on the following day, Tuesday, December 29th, they rode to Canterbury with a small company of armed followers. These men they left in a house near the palace gate, and having deposited their own weapons outside, they demanded audience of the Archbishop.

It was then about the middle of the afternoon, and the usual three o'clock repast in the great hall was ended. Becket had gone to his own rooms, and here he received the knights. The interview was stormy. The four men called loudly for the absolution of the bishops, the Archbishop recited his own wrongs, both sides threatened the other. The noise attracted a number of monks and servants, who rushed to defend their master, and the knights. who could do nothing at the moment because they were unarmed. withdrew to fetch their weapons and summon their followers. The monks meanwhile urged Becket to take refuge in the cathedral. He refused, and it was then that John of Salisbury made his pathetic reproach. To all representations of his imminent danger the Archbishop replied simply that God's will would be done, and it was only when he was reminded that it was now the hour of vespers, which it was his duty to attend, that he consented to leave his room and go to the Cathedral.

The outer court was by this time thronged with armed men, and the ordinary approach to the church was impassable. The little band of monks, therefore, went through a private door which led into the cloisters. It was here that the first occurrence afterwards looked upon as a miracle took place. The door was bolted on the wrong side and could not be opened, but when an attempt was made to force it, it flew open without the exercise of any strength. Nearly all the chroniclers of the time record this incident as miraculous, except Benedict, afterwards Abbot of Peterborough, and at that time a monk of Canterbury. His explanation is simple. Two cellarmen who lived on the premises, hearing the uproar without, had the presence of mind to remember the private door and rushed to unbolt it from the other side. The terrified monks passed through without seeing their benefactors, the Archbishop walking with unhurried dignity and his cross-bearer going before him, as on ordinary occasions. Finally the impatient clerics were reduced to dragging and pushing their master, much against his will, in a vain effort to make him hasten to the only place where he had a reasonable chance of safety.

In the Cathedral itself Becket refused to allow the great door to be barred, though the armed men were already in the cloisters. Only with difficulty was he persuaded to ascend the flight of steps leading to the choir, and while he was yet mounting them, the four knights rushed into the transept. Becket at once descended and stood between the central pillar and the wall. And here he was killed. The murderers, either from a deep-seated aversion to shedding blood in a church, or from fear of rescue, tried to drag him outside, but setting his back against the pillar he resisted with all his might. He was a strong man, and in the ensuing struggle he flung William de Tracy to the ground. Most of the monks had already fled, but one, Edward Grim, tried to shield him from his adversaries' repeated blows and was wounded in the arm. Finally Becket fell, and as he lay on the ground Richard le Bret struck him with such force that his scalp was severed from his head and the knight's sword broken in two. Seeing their victim was at last dead the murderers hastily left the church and went to the private rooms, where they seized a number of papers; afterwards they plundered the palace. As they left the precincts a violent storm burst over Canterbury, and this was followed about midnight by the unusual and, in the circumstances, terrifying appearance of the Aurora Borealis.

During all this time many people had been present in the

St. Thomas à Becket: Saint, Hero, and Martyr

cathedral or the precincts and had been more or less helpless spectators of the struggle in the transept. News of the tragedy spread rapidly through the town, and crowds flocked to the desecrated church. All were horrified at the sacrilege, but not all as yet believed the dead prelate to be a martyr for his religion. Even in his own city there were some who sided with the King and regarded his death, however dreadful its accompanying circumstances, as a deserved execution rather than an assassination. But the sight of the broken corpse, the blood and brains spattered over the sacred stones, and the hair-shirt worn by the victim in mute testimony of his piety, confirmed the majority in the belief that he was a true saint and martyr. They dipped their clothes into his blood, and one man, taking his shirt so stained home to his paralytic wife, soaked it in water and gave her the resulting liquid to drink. She was immediately cured. Many believed the crimson streamers of the Aurora Borealis to be the Archbishop's blood ascending to Heaven; the exhausted monks who watched by his body swore, and no doubt believed, that in the first light of the winter dawn they had seen the dead man raise his hand and bless them with the sign of the Cross. All Becket's benefactions to the poor, the curious stories told about his visions, and his apparent expectation of martyrdom, his dignity and courage, and his undaunted struggle for what he believed to be right were remembered on that awful night, and henceforward few doubted that a new glory had been added to the Church in England.

On the following day the body was secretly buried in the crypt for fear of de Broc, who is said to have forbidden the monks to lay it beside the former prelates in the Cathedral. A wooden altar was set up on the spot where he died, and the place was afterwards known as The Martyrdom. It was this altar, which did not exist in his lifetime, that seems to have given rise to the tradition that Becket was murdered, suddenly and without warning, whilst quietly praying before it. A great devotion to the new martyr now sprang up. Pilgrims flocked to the Cathedral and were given flasks containing drops of his blood diluted with water; the possession of such a flask became the sign of a Canterbury pilgrim, as a scallop shell was of a pilgrimage to Compostella. Three years later

Pope Alexander III, after sending legates to investigate the accounts of numerous miracles, confirmed the popular verdict by canonizing the dead archbishop and setting aside December 29th as his Feast Day.

Of the many peculiar circumstances of his murder, two especially impressed his contemporaries. One was the day on which it occurred, the other his clear expectation of it. It was, of course, merely coincidence that he died on a Tuesday, for no one could possibly have anticipated Henry's ill-omened words or the date on which they would be uttered, and once heard, they were acted upon by the four knights with the least possibly delay. But Tuesday had always been an important day in Becket's life, and few failed to remark the fatality which made it important to the very end. On a Tuesday he was born and baptized. On that day of the week he left Northampton after his furious defiance of the King and council. On one Tuesday his exile began, and on another, six years later, it ended. Long afterwards his remains were to be translated on a Tuesday from their first resting-place to the newly erected shrine. Moreover, it was on such a day that he is said to have seen a vision at Pontigny, warning him of martyrdom to come.

That he anticipated a martyr's fate and did not shrink from it is evident. Before his return to England he told several people that he would not survive the year's end, a somewhat curious prophecy in view of the fact that he had made his peace with the King and should, therefore, have had little to fear from that quarter. It is true that the reconciliation, at least on his side, was hollow from the start, since he had no intention of abating one jot of his claims, and no visions or second-sight were needed to warn him that trouble could not be far distant. Nevertheless, as he only reached England in December, the time he allowed himself was very short. On his last visit to his manor-house at Harrow he had told the Abbot of St. Albans that "the days of the end hasten to their completion", which may or may not have had a reference to his own end, and very shortly afterwards, on Christmas Day, he spoke of another martyr for Canterbury to his congregation and again to his cross-bearer. On the morning of December 29th he told those surrounding him that any who wished to escape might do so; at dinner he drank more than usual and explained it by the strange remark that those who had much blood to shed must drink much.

An extraordinary atmosphere seems to have brooded over Canterbury in those last days. Monks dreamed of the archbishop's approaching death, and one, William of Canterbury, tells us that Becket "knew that the sword threatened his head, and the time was at hand for his sacrifice." When the danger was actually upon him, he refused to make any real effort to save himself. In the hands of his murderers he declared himself ready to die, and only began to struggle when they attempted to drag him out of the church. Tradition has it that his death was known in Jerusalem on the same night. In Devonshire a child of seven, after sitting silent for some time at the dinner-table told his family that a good priest had just that moment been killed. Similar stories were told after the murder of William Rufus, whom no one regarded as a saint. In his case also the news was known in Devonshire on the very day of his death, and was told to Peter de Melvis by a stranger even before it was generally known in Winchester, to which town the body was taken by the charcoal burner who found it.

Folk-legend ascribed a hard fate to the murderers, who were popularly supposed to have led unhappy lives and to have died early by violence or painful disease. On leaving Canterbury they rode to Saltwood and thence to South Malling, on their way to Knaresborough Castle which was then held by Hugh de Moreville. At Malling they laid their arms upon a table in the hall, but the inanimate wood refused to bear the bloodstained burden and twice flung it to the ground. Thenceforward, according to tradition, they were cursed. The very dogs refused to take food from their hands, and nothing that they did prospered. Three died fighting in the Holy Land, where they were sent by the Pope to expiate their crime, but de Tracy, who struck the first blow, was never able to reach that country. The wind blew persistently against his ship, and he died miserably at Cosenza of an agonizing disease. The curse descended in a milder form to all his family, and as late as last century a Gloucestershire proverb declared that "The Tracies have always the wind in their faces."

In fact, very little seems to have happened to them. That they did penance is extremely probable, for they were all excommunicated shortly after the murder, and some expiation they must have made to free themselves from that dire penalty. They may actually have visited the Holy Land for this purpose. But no secular punishment was inflicted on them, and in the existing confused state of the law concerning the relations of clerics and laymen, it does not seem that any such punishment could have been imposed. They appear to have retained their lands and position, and two years after Becket's death they were again at court and about the King's person. William de Tracy is known to have been Justiciary of Normandy in 1174. Fitzurse seems to have retired to Ireland and is said to have founded a family there. History records little more of Richard le Bret's affairs, but no untoward fate appears to have overtaken him, and he was able to transmit his estates peacefully to his daughter when he died. In later years Alice, his granddaughter, gave lands to the Priory of Woodspring in the hope that the intercession of the glorious martyr, St. Thomas, might never be wanting to her and her children. Hugh de Moreville died quietly in the early years of King John's reign, having become very wealthy in the interval. His part in the tragedy had been less violent than that of the others, though he cannot be considered any less guilty than they. He was the only one who tried to show some courtesy to Becket during the preliminary interview, and later, in the Cathedral, he had no share in the actual murder, being occupied in guarding the entrance to the transept and holding off those who tried to come to the Archbishop's help.

It was the King who suffered the worst consequences of the crime which his ill-judged words had inspired. The news of the murder threw him into a frenzy of grief. He shut himself away in solitude for three days, refusing all food and calling continuously upon God to witness that he was not responsible for what had happened. For several weeks afterwards he transacted no public business and passed his time in fruitless lamentation. Meanwhile his enemies hastened to denounce him to the Pope and to demand his punishment by personal excommunication and an interdict upon England. The threat of these terrible penalties roused him from his mourning, and he took immediate steps to avert them by submission. From the beginning he had strenuously denied that he had ever intended his words to be taken seriously, and now he took an oath to this effect at Avranches. In the presence of the Council and the Papal Legate he asserted his innocence of all desire for the Archbishop's death; he acknowledged that his wild utterances had been the first cause of the crime and declared his readiness, since he could not put the actual murderers to death, to render personally whatever satisfaction the Pope might demand.

Four years later he made an even more definite avowal of repentance by a public penance in Canterbury. At this period his fortunes were at a very low ebb. The King of Scotland had invaded the northern counties, Yorkshire, Norfolk and the Midlands were all in open rebellion, and his own sons had joined the ranks of his enemies. The mainspring of these revolts was, of course, political, but hostility to the King was greatly strengthened, at least amongst the ordinary people by the widespread devotion to St. Thomas of Canterbury and the memory of Henry's share in his death. The solemn oath sworn at Avranches had not been enough to clear him altogether in the eyes of his subjects, in spite of the absolution received on that occasion. So, in a final endeavour to prove his real penitence, if not his actual innocence, he made, in July 1174, one of the most spectacular and impressive gestures ever performed by a king in the Middle Ages.

Putting off every sign and appearance of royalty, he walked, barefoot and clad only in a woollen shirt and a cloak, through the streets of Canterbury from St. Dunstan's Church to the Cathedral, where he knelt first in the transept and kissed the stone upon which the martyr had fallen. Then, going into the crypt, he knelt before the tomb and was scourged by the bishops and monks assembled there. Throughout the night he lay fasting on the bare ground of the crypt; in the morning, after hearing Mass, he returned to London, where he succumbed to a violent fever, brought on by exhaustion and nervous strain. Such public humiliations had, of course, been voluntarily suffered by other kings in earlier ages, but none had taken place for many years before his time, and the impression made upon his contemporaries was very

great. Moreover, as the devout were quick to record, his reconciliation with the martyred archbishop was followed immediately
by a great change in his fortunes. Gervase of Canterbury tells
us that four days after his return he was roused from sleep by
the news that William the Lion, King of Scotland, had been
defeated and taken prisoner on the very day that Henry had left
Canterbury after his penance. Nor was this all, for on that day
also the fleet in which Prince Henry had hoped to invade his
father's dominions was scattered and driven back to Flanders.
The King's troubles were now at least temporarily at an end,
and to the people of that time it was clear that his share in the
archbishop's murder had been forgiven alike by God and by his
victim.

For more than three hundred years thereafter St. Thomas of
Canterbury lived on in the hearts of the people as one of the hero-
saints of England. To his magnificent shrine in the Cathedral
flocked innumerable pilgrims from his own and other countries.
Many churches and monastic buildings bore his name, including
the chapel that guarded London Bridge and the Priory of Woodspring, which was built by William de Tracy's grandson in expiation of his grandfather's crime. From the front of Lambeth Palace
his statue looked over the Thames and was saluted daily by all the
watermen as they passed up and down the river. His penknife was
preserved at Bury, his boots at Windsor, his girdle at Chester.
When John Colet, Dean of St. Paul's Cathedral, visited Canterbury
in the early sixteenth century, an aged almsman at Harbledown
offered him St. Thomas's shoe to kiss, to his great and violently
expressed disgust. Nor was the cult confined to England, for many
European churches were dedicated to the martyr, or contained his
relics. At Sens his vestments were kept in the cathedral; at Verona
the church of San Thomaso Cantuariense contained his tooth, and
at Chartres a window depicted the story of his stormy life. There
was a chapel dedicated to him at Fourrieres, and another in Rome.
During the Crusades an Englishman vowed to build a chapel in
his name if he entered Acre in safety, and this vow was fulfilled.
Richard I also founded an order of St. Thomas there under the
control of the Knights Templars. Hence he was often known
as St. Thomas of Acre, or Thomas Acrensis, and this was the

dedication of the chapel built in London to mark the place where he was born.

A host of miracles was ascribed to his intercession, or to the blood which the monks had gathered up on the night of his death. In 1370 Simon of Sudbury, then Bishop of London, sinned against the popular hero-worship by speaking slightingly of the saint's powers to a number of pilgrims. There was an immediate outcry. Many cursed the Bishop, and one man prophesied that he would die a terrible death. When, in fact, he did so, being butchered by Wat Tyler's followers during the rebellion of 1381, many believed that the vengeance of St. Thomas had overtaken him at last. In later years a well in the precincts of Canterbury Cathedral was pointed out as the place where the bloodstained dust of the transept had been thrown after the murder. This well had previously provided only a meagre supply of water, but when the dust was thrown into it, it became a full-flowing spring. Many cures were wrought by its waters. On several occasions it was said to run with blood, and once with milk. This legend was unknown to early chroniclers, and seems to have been first told in the reign of Edward II, perhaps as the result of a reddish tinge in the water due to the presence of some mineral. But the later monks and pilgrims believed it fervently, and the miraculous well was visited almost as often as the shrine itself.

When the Reformation came, St. Thomas's cult suffered with that of other saints, and, indeed, more than most. Henry VIII is said to have had a special enmity to this turbulent martyr whose ideal of a Church entirely independent of the State was the exact opposite of all for which Henry stood. In 1538 the great shrine was destroyed and its jewels and gold carried away. The Archbishop's bones were scattered or, according to another account, mingled with those of others in such a way that they could never again be distinguished. In the same year the King made his particular detestation of St. Thomas apparent by issuing a proclamation in which Becket's death was described, with special emphasis on the evidences of his headstrong character, and the whole incident was given the appearance of a fatal brawl rather than a martyrdom. It went on to say that "there appeareth nothing in his life or exterior conversation whereby he could be called a saint but rather esteemed a rebel and traitor to his prince. Therefore his Grace straightly chargeth and commandeth that henceforth the said Thomas Becket shall not be esteemed, named, reputed nor called a saint but 'Bishop Becket', and that his images and pictures throughout the whole realm shall be put down and avoided out of all churches and chapels and other places . . ."

These commands were strictly obeyed. The saint's memorials disappeared from the churches. The arms of the City of Canterbury were altered; the pilgrimages ceased. The site of the destroyed shrine was left vacant, and the crypt where his bones had first rested was used as a wine-cellar. His statues and pictures were torn down, illuminated books illustrating his life were defaced. In Oxford Cathedral, where the east window of St. Lucy's Chapel depicted the martyrdom, the archbishop's head was obliterated and the space filled with a piece of white glass. The shrines of all the saints suffered at this period, but the memory of St. Thomas was subjected to a more deadly and systematic attack than the rest, for the animus behind it was political as well as ecclesiastical. Henry II was thus at long last avenged upon his enemy by his descendant. In spite of the King's edict, St. Thomas remained one of the saints of the Church, but his special cult in England was ended. Once its central shrine was destroyed, the great devotion that had blossomed for three centuries faded quickly from the minds of all but the very devout. There were no folk-plays or ballads to remind the people of Becket, as they were reminded of St. George; nor were his own undoubted virtues of that chivalric and self-denying kind that could preserve his name in later ages, as St. George's name was preserved, as a type of Christian strength and courage. Henceforth the reverence paid to him was simply that paid to many other saints and martyrs, or to great historical figures; he no longer reigned as a living force in the hearts of ordinary men, and had ceased to be a hero of the folk.

BIBLIOGRAPHY

Addy, S.O.: *Church & Manor*, 1913.

Anglo-Saxon Chronicle: (ed. J. Earle & C. Plummer, 1892–9).

Asser, Bishop: *Life of Alfred* (ed. W. H. Stevenson, 1904).

Baring-Gould, S.: *A Book of the West*, 1899; *Curious Myths of the Middle Ages*, 1869.

Bede, The Venerable: *Ecclesiastical History of England* (ed. J. A. Giles, 1859).

Borlase, W.: *Antiquities of Cornwall*, 1754.

Brabrook, Sir E.: "Robin Hood", article in *The Antiquary*. Vol. 42. 1906.

Brand, J.: *Observations on the Popular Antiquities of Great Britain* (ed. Sir Henry Ellis, 1849).

Brome, J.: *Travels over England, Scotland and Wales*, 1700.

Bruce, Dr. Collingwood: *Wallet Book of the Roman Wall*, 1863.

Burne, C. S.: *Shropshire Folklore*, 1883.

Camden, W.: *Britannia:* Newly Translated into English with large Additions & Improvements. Published by Edward Gibson of Queen's College, Oxford, 1695.

Carew, R.: *Survey of Cornwall*, 1602.

Chambers, Sir E. K.: *Arthur of Britain*, 1928; *The English Folk-Play*, 1933.

Chambers, R.: *The Book of Days*, 1864.

Chambers, R. W.: *England Before the Norman Conquest*, 1928.

Charlton, L.: *A History of Whitby and of Whitby Abbey*, 1779.

Collingwood, R. G. & Myres, J. N. L.: *Roman Britain and the English Settlements*, 1936.

Conybeare, Edward: *History of Cambridgeshire*, 1897.

Denham, M.: *The Denham Tracts* (ed. Dr. J. Hardy, 1892, 1895).

Dickenson, W. H.: *King Arthur in Cornwall*, 1900.

Dictionary of National Biography.

Dugdale, Sir William: *Monasticon Anglicanum*, 1817–30.

Elton, C.: *Origins of English History*, 1890.

BIBLIOGRAPHY

Finny, Dr. W. E.: *Mediæval Games and Gaderyngs at Kingston-upon-Thames*, 1936.

Fordun, J.: *Scotichronicon* (ed. W. F. Skene, 1871–2).

Freeman, A.: *History of the Norman Conquest*, 1870–6.

Froissart, J.: *Chroniques* (ed. T. Johnes, 1844).

Fuller, Dr.: *History of the Worthies of England*, 1662.

Geoffrey of Monmouth: *Historia Regum Britanniæ* (ed. J. A. Giles, 1866).

Gildas: *Liber de Excidio et Conquestu Britanniæ* (ed J. A. Giles, 1866).

Glennie, J. Stuart: *Arthurian Localities*, 1869.

Gomme, G. L.: *Ethnology in Folklore*, 1892; *Folklore as an Historical Science*, 1908.

Gwynn Jones, T.: *Welsh Folklore and Folk Custom*, 1930.

Hardwick, C.: *Traditions, Superstitions and Folklore*, 1872.

Harland, J. & Wilkinson, T.: *Lancashire Folklore*, 1867.

Hartland, E. S.: *The Science of Fairy-Tales*, 1891.

Henderson, W.: *Notes on the Folklore of the Northern Counties of England and the Borders*, 1879.

Herbert, W. I.: *The History of the Twelve Great Livery Companies*, 1834–7.

Hodgson, J.: *History of Northumberland*, 1840.

Hole, C.: *Traditions and Customs of Cheshire*, 1937.

Hope, C.: *Holy Wells: Their Legends and Traditions*, 1893.

Hunt, R.: *Popular Romances of the West of England*, 1865. 1881.

Hunter, J.: *Critical and Historical Tracts*, No. IV. 1852.

Keightley, J.: *The Fairy Mythology*, 1850.

Kitteredge, G. L.: *Witchcraft in Old and New England*, 1929.

Knox, Fr. R. & Leslie, Shane: *The Miracles of King Henry VI*, 1923.

Leather, E. A.: *The Folklore of Herefordshire*, 1912.

Lewis Jones, W.: *King Arthur in History and Legend*, 1933.

Mabinogion, The: trans. Lady Guest (ed. A. Nutt), 1904.

Maitland, T.: *History and Chronicles of Scotland*, 1821.

Malory, T.: *Morte d'Arthur* (ed. H. O. Sommer, 1889–91).

Marcus, G. J.: *St. George of England*, 1929.

McCulloch, J. A.: *Mediæval Faith and Fable*, 1932.

Murray, M. A.: *The God of the Witches*, 1933.

Nennius: *Historia Britonnum* (ed. J. A. Giles, 1866).

176

BIBLIOGRAPHY

Nichols, J.: *History of Leicestershire*, 1795.

Oman, Sir Charles: *England Before the Norman Conquest*, 1910.

Paston Letters: (ed. Dr. Gairdiner, 1904).

Parkinson, T.: *Yorkshire Legends and Traditions*, 1889.

Pearson, W.: *Antiquities of Salop*, 1824.

Raine, J.: *Historians of the Church of York* (R.S.), 1879.

Rees, J. Aubrey: *The English Tradition*, 1934.

Ritson, J.: *Robin Hood*, 1795.

Robertson, J. C.: *Materials for the Life of Thomas à Becket*, 1859.

Robinson, J. Armitage: *Somerset Historical Essays*, 1912; *Two Glastonbury Legends*, 1926.

Roger of Wendover: *Flores Historiarum* (ed. J. A. Giles, 1849).

Rudder, Samuel: *A New History of Gloucestershire*, 1779.

Rye, Walter: *History of Norfolk*, 1885.

Shirley, Hon. R.: "Arthur of Britain": article in *The Cornhill Magazine*, July 1939.

Snell, F. J.: *King Arthur's Country*, 1926.

Stanley, A. P.: *Historical Memorials of Canterbury*, 1906.

Stapleton, A.: *Robin Hood: The Question of his Existence*, 1899.

Stow, J.: *Annales*, 1605; *Survey of London* (ed. Rev. J. Strype), 1755.

Tiddy, R. J. E.: *The Mummers' Play*, 1923.

Thoroton, R.: *History of Nottinghamshire*, (ed. J. Throsby, 1790).

Urlin, E.: *Festivals, Holy Days, & Saints' Days*.

Voragine, J. de: *The Golden Legend* (Temple Classics).

William of Malmesbury: *De Rebus Gestis Regum Anglorum* (ed. W. Stubbs), (R.S.).

Wood, Mrs. F. S.: *Somerset Memories and Traditions*, 1924.

Wright, T.: *Essays on Subjects Connected with the Literature, Popular Superstitions and History of England in the Middle Ages*, 1846.

Young, George: *A History of Whitby and Streoneshalh Abbey*, 1817.

County Folklore: *Leicestershire and Rutland* (ed. C. J. Billson), 1895; *North Riding of Yorkshire, York and the Ainsty* (ed. Mrs. Gutch), 1901; *Northumberland* (ed. Mrs. Balfour), 1904; *Suffolk* (ed. Lady C. Gurdon), 1893.

Antiquary, The, 1906.

BIBLIOGRAPHY

Archælogia Cantiæ (Publications of the Kent Archæological Society).

Cheshire Sheaf, The.

Folklore.

Folklore Record, The.

Gentleman's Magazine Library.

Gloucestershire Notes and Queries.

Leicestershire Notes and Queries.

Lincolnshire Notes and Queries.

Palatine Notebook.

Proceedings of the Hampshire Field Club.

Proceedings of the Somerset Archæological and Natural History Society.

Somerset and Dorset Notes and Queries.

Suffolk Garland, The.

Suffolk Notes and Queries.

Transactions of the Devonshire Association.

Transactions of the Lancashire and Cheshire Antiquarian Society.

Yorkshire Notes and Queries.

INDEX

INDEX

INDEX

INDEX

This book may be kept

FOURTEEN DAYS

A fine will be charged for each day the book is kept overtime.

3-1604			
		.	
GAYLORD 142			PRINTED IN U.S.A.